COMMUNICATING WITH OLDER ADULTS

A Guide for Health Care and Senior Service Professionals and Staff

Ann E. Benbow, Ph.D.
Director, Adult Learning and Technology
The SPRY Foundation

NCPSSM

CARESOURCE
HEALTHCARE COMMUNICATIONS

SeniorClix.com

Library of Congress Cataloging-in-Publication Data

Benbow, Ann.
  Communicating with older adults : a guide for health care and senior service professionals and staff / Ann E. Benbow.
      p. cm.
    ISBN 1-878866-20-6
    1. Medical personnel and patient. 2. Aged—Communication.
  3. Communication in medicine. I. Title.
    R727.3 .B454 2002
    618.97'0233—dc21

                                        2002010908

Cover illustration by Zanetka Kral
Cover and publication design by Colleen Schlonga

Caresource Healthcare Communications, Inc.
426 Yale Avenue N
Seattle, WA 98109
www.caresource.com

Distributed in association with Conifer Publishing, Seattle, WA

ACKNOWLEDGMENTS

This publication could not have been completed without the important contributions made by organizations and individuals from across the United States.

First, we would like to acknowledge Marilyn Hennessy and the Retirement Research Foundation, which provided the vision and funding to make this publication possible.

We would also like to thank the following individuals who took time to review and validate the draft materials: Dr. Elliot Abt, Director of the Dental Residency Program at Advocate/Illinois Masonic Medical Center (Chicago, Illinois); Dr. Martin Bascove, Attending Physician at the Veterans Administration Hospital (West Palm Beach, Florida); Sandra Bascove, RPh, Pharmacist and Pharmacy Manager at Eckerts Pharmacy (Palm Beach Gardens, Florida); Dr. Robert Brown, Leadership Development Consultant (Rockville, Maryland); Dr. James C. Burden, D.M.D., Bur-Dent Services (Howell, New Jersey); Mary Ann Cook, Ph.D., Owner of JVC Radiology and Medical Analysis, LLC (St. Louis, Missouri); Jayson M. Dupre, D.O., Chief Medical Resident at the Lehigh Valley Hospital (Allentown, Pennsylvania); Dalia Garrett, RN, MSN, CS, Geriatric Nurse Practitioner (Frankfort, Illinois); Christine M. Grant, J.D., MBA, Vice President of Aventis Pasteur, Inc. (Swiftwater, Pennsylvania); Lorayne Warber Hrejsa, RN, BSN, MS, Manager Education and Accreditation at the Dreyer Medical Clinic (Batavia, Illinois); Concha Johnson, Executive Director of Senior Citizens Counseling and Delivery Services (Washington, DC); Robert Kahn, Ph.D., Professor Emeritus of Psychology and Public Health at the University of Michigan (Ann Arbor, Michigan); Moon Ju Kim, RN, FNP, Nurse Practitioner at the Center for Healthy Aging (Santa Monica, California); Amy Liston, Ph.D., Caregiver Services Coordinator at the Center for Healthy Aging (Santa Monica, California); Donna L. Miller, DO, Medical Director of the Geriatric Institute, St. Luke's Hospital and Health Network (Bethlehem, Pennsylvania); Russell E. Morgan, Sr., M.D.; Dr. Jennifer Neuendorff, Family Practitioner at Southside Family Medicine (Allentown, Pennsylvania); Jerry Neece, Strategic Programs Manager of Worldwide Education and Research at Sun Microsystems (Palo Alto, California); Eva M. Lauter, BSN, MSN, Lauter & Associates (Washington, DC); Joyce Rosenblum, MA, MFT, Physician Liaison at the Center for Healthy Aging (Santa Monica, California); Sheila Segal, MA, MFT, Clinical Coordinator Peer Counseling at the Center for Healthy Aging (Santa Monica, California); and Dr. Chris Vojta, Vice President and Medical Director of Intracorp (Philadelphia, Pennsylvania).

We would like to thank those who helped identify reviewers for this project, including Brian M. Duke, M.H.A., Director of Geriatric Program Initiatives at the University of Pennsylvania Health System Institute on Aging; Patti Ludwig-Beymer, Ph.D., RN, Research and Education Administrator at Advocate Health Care in Oak Brook, Illinois; and Monika White, Ph.D., President and CEO of the Center for Healthy Aging in Santa Monica, California.

Alma Strack, Assistant Director of the Monmouth County, New Jersey Office on Aging provided invaluable input on recommended practices for senior Information and Referral Specialists. We are also grateful to Bob Bernoff, Ph.D., Emeritus Professor of Science and General Chemistry at the Pennsylvania State University who provided invaluable assistance as the evaluator of the project.

Finally, we would like to thank Amy Harshfield, research assistant; Mary Pershing and EEI Communications for copy editing this publication, and Marina Herrera for translating this publication into Spanish.

ERRATUM

In Chapters 1 through 4, under the subsections titled "Details on Checklist Items," there is a discrepancy between the **Research Base** references and the actual page numbers on which they appear. Each "Older Adult Learning Factor" is located two pages later than the page number indicated (i.e., **Research Base: Self-directed Learning, p. 70** should be **Research Base: Self-directed Learning, p. 72**). The correct pages for each "Older Adult Learning Factor" are as follows:

CONTENTS

INTRODUCTION

Purpose

The purpose of this handbook is to provide health care professionals with research-based guidance on how they can communicate more efficiently and effectively with older adults.

Older Adults, a Definition

For the purposes of this guide, older adults are defined as people aged 55 and older who are not suffering from any forms of dementia. The communications techniques suggested in this guide are for average adults in this age group who, although possibly affected by some decline in their physical and mental abilities, are still able to function. We recognize that there is great diversity in the physical and mental states of individuals in this age group.

Reason for the Guide

The vanguard of the "baby boom" generation is on the verge of reaching retirement age. This means that, over the next decade, a much greater percentage of the U.S. population will be "older adults" (55+) than ever before. This aging population will increase the overall need in the United States for good health education, health care, information about medications, caregiver services, and much more.

The people on the front line for providing this information and care are you, the health care and senior service professionals. Unfortunately, the time available for working with patients and clients is shrinking as the population of older adults is growing. One of the goals of this guide is to help you maximize the effectiveness of the time you do spend with older adults. The guide is designed to help you understand some of the learning preferences of older adults and use these to enhance communication, increase compliance, and build trust with your clients and patients.

Genesis of the Guide

This guide was developed by the SPRY (Setting Priorities for Retirement Years) Foundation, with funding from the Retirement Research Foundation. SPRY is a nonprofit group in Washington, DC, that engages in research and education projects that promote the concept of Successful Aging. The guide is based upon the research that the SPRY Foundation conducted in 1999 on how older adults learn and make decisions. This research, entitled *Bridging Principles of Older Adult Learning*, was a meta-analysis co-sponsored by the SPRY Foundation and the Robert Wood Johnson Foundation.

The project examined over 300 journal articles concerning older adult learning, looking for areas of agreement among researchers. The studies analyzed were from the fields of education, neuroscience, psychology, gerontology, communications technology, adult literacy and marketing. In addition to the meta-analysis, the study included interviews with 129 professionals in the field of older adult learning. The results of these interviews were also included in the data analysis.

The outcome of this research project was a set of proposed principles of older adult learning. These principles were the result of strong areas of agreement among researchers. It is upon these areas of agreement that this guide is based.

Highlights of Research Findings

Here are a few of the findings from the *Bridging Principles* study:

From the Medical Sciences:

- Stimulating environments have been linked to the continued growth of older adult brain cells, and to learning and memory.

  (Normal aging does not always involve significant cognitive decline and dementia.)

- Older adult brains have a high degree of plasticity and the ability to rebound following trauma.

(The adult brain does not have a fixed capacity that declines with age, reducing learning ability.)

From Adult Education:

- Older adults use their experience, skills, and knowledge in processing new information and making decisions.

    (Older adults know where to get additional information; they have a network of social structures and friends that assists with their learning and decision-making.)

- Third-party validation helps older adults make decisions.

    (The use of legitimate "authority/trust" persons – family members, neighbors, nurses, etc. – provides a basis for learning and decision-making that can be important.)

From Communication Technologies:

- New technologies can facilitate the ability of older adults to learn new information.

    (Computer/Internet-based learning can be customized or specially designed to meet an individual's learning style and needs.)

- New technologies allow tremendous flexibility and power in adapting the learning environment to the capacity of the older individual.

    (Internet technologies can be designed to adapt to the sensory needs and memory strategies of older adults, as well as to their learning methods at each step in a training program.)

This guide takes each finding that has implications for communicating with older adults in health care settings and explains how the finding plays out in practice.

How this Book is Organized

Section I contains five checklists of suggested techniques arranged chronologically to fit most clinical settings. These communication techniques are appropriate for use by physicians, nurses, dentists, or other medical professionals. After each checklist is a subsection providing details on how to implement the suggestion in the checklist. The five checklists are:

- *Before the Office Visit:* Contacts with patients/clients before an office visit.

- *At the Office, Before the Consultation:* Contacts with office staff and materials in the waiting room that are available to patients/clients before they see the medical professional. This section includes interactions with a medical assistant before the consultation actually begins.

- *Beginning the Consultation:* Discussion prior to any physical examination.

- *Continuing the Consultation:* Discussions during the main body of the consultation.

- *Ending the Consultation:* Discussions at the end of the consultation that include follow-up items (prescriptions, directions, advice, contact information).

Section I also contains templates and forms that can help health care professionals implement some of the suggestions in this book.

Section II contains two checklists of suggested techniques for use in pharmacy settings. These communication techniques are appropriate for use by pharmacists and pharmacy technicians. After each checklist is a subsection providing details on how to implement the suggestion in the checklist. The two checklists are:

- *Informational Materials:* Suggestions about types of materials that might be most effective with and user-friendly for older adult customers.

- *Face-to-Face Interactions:* Practical suggestions on how to discuss medications most effectively with older adult customers and how to answer their questions with care and sensitivity.

Section II also contains a survey form that can help pharmacy professionals implement some of the suggestions in the guide.

Section III contains three checklists of suggested techniques for use in communicating with and serving mentally competent residents and patients in assisted living, sub-acute and rehab care settings, and nursing homes. (Note, however, that these techniques are NOT intended for use in situations involving patients or residents who are suffering from Alzheimer's disease or other forms of dementia.) After each checklist is a subsection providing details on how to implement the suggestion in the checklist. The three checklists are:

- *Informational Materials:* Suggestions about types of materials that may be the most user-friendly and beneficial for residents.

- *Working One-on-One with Residents:* Practical suggestions on how to work with residents in helping them to comply with their medical regimens and in their activities of daily living.

- *Working with Residents and Health Care Professionals:* Suggestions and ideas for how to maximize the effectiveness of the time that residents spend with visiting health care professionals.

Also included at the close of Section III is a survey form that can help staff in assisted living communities and rehab and skilled nursing facilities implement some of the suggestions presented in this book.

Section IV contains four checklists of suggested techniques for use with older adult clients. These communication techniques are appropriate for use by Information and Referral Specialists in a variety of settings. After each checklist is a subsection providing details on how to implement the suggestion in the checklist. The subsections are:

- *Informational Materials:* Suggestions about types of materials that may be the most user-friendly and beneficial for older adult clients.

- *Working Face-to-Face with Clients:* Practical suggestions on how to work with clients in helping them to find the information and help they need to stay as independent as they can for as long as possible.

- *Working with Clients and Health Care Professionals:* Suggestions and ideas for how to maximize the effectiveness of the time that clients spend with their health care professionals.

- *Talking on the Telephone with Clients:* Advice on how to maximize interactions with older adult clients over the telephone.

Section IV also contains forms that can help Information and Referral Specialists implement some of the suggestions in the guide.

Section V summarizes the research findings of the SPRY/RWJF research project. The research is presented as a set of 19 learning factors appropriately considered in communicating with and providing care to older adults. The section also includes a list of additional resources for each of the 19 learning factors, as well as source citations for each of the 19.

The **Appendix** is a table comparing the strategies used by older learners and younger learners.

Finally, there are **Profiles** of Dr. Ann Benbow, The SPRY Foundation, and Caresource.

I.
Recommended Practices for Healthcare Professionals and Clinical Care Workers

This section of the guide provides guidance for health care professionals who work in clinical settings. The information in this section provides practical suggestions for improving communication with older adult patients and clients by using the findings from research into older adult learning.

The goal of this part of the guide is to maximize the effectiveness of the time spent with older adult patients to make them feel: comfortable and accepted; cared for and informed; and confident that they are receiving appropriate treatment and advice for their needs, ages, and circumstances.

Checklist: Before the Office Visit

Before the Office Visit

1. Send a letter to patients to help them prepare for the office visit.

2. Encourage patients to bring along a family member or trusted friend.

3. If appropriate, encourage patients to bring an audiotape recorder.

4. Help the patient to set up an appointment/medication reminder system that works for him or her.

5. If email and the World Wide Web are important to your practice, make patients aware of computer training opportunities in your community.

Details on Checklist Items

1. Send a letter to patients to help them prepare for the office visit.

A letter sent home before the office visit can help older adult patients and their caregivers to collect and focus on their questions and concerns. The letter can contain such information as the following:

- How you typically conduct an office visit

- How long the visit usually takes

- The type of information you typically request from a patient

- Appropriate times in the visit for questions and answers.

The letter can also make these suggestions to help the patient prepare for the visit (as appropriate):

- Writing down important questions in advance

- Inviting a family member or friend to come along on the office visit

- Tracking a symptom and keeping notes on it

- Remembering to bring in current medications

- Keeping and bringing in a record of his or her weight

- Keeping and bringing in a record of what he or she typically eats in a day

- Reflecting on recent events in his or her life that might have implications on physical or mental health

- Remembering to bring in old medical records (if a new patient).

Note: Make sure that the letter is in a large font.

Research Base: A Focus on the Issues, p. 69

2. Encourage patients to bring along a family member or trusted friend.

As stated in #1 above, many older adults benefit by having a family member or trusted friend accompany them to an office visit. The family member can assist in a variety of ways:

- Remind the patient of important questions that need to be discussed.

- Participate in hands-on training when the patient is learning a new technique or how to use a new device during the office visit.

- Take notes on what the patient is supposed to do after the visit.

- Provide comfort to a patient in the case of bad news during the visit.

- Provide additional information about the patient's home environment.

In the case of hands-on training, the family member can provide the older adult with a back-up system in case he or she is still unsure about the procedure after leaving the office. You can also provide written directions that support the hands-on experience and refer to these directions during the training.

Research Base: Social Learning Context, p. 71; Desire for Hands-On Learning, p. 74; Request for Memory Prompts, p. 75; Opportunity for Reflection, p. 82

3. If appropriate, encourage patients to bring an audiotape recorder.

Depending upon what is appropriate for you and your practice, you might want to recommend that older adult patients, particularly those who are reluctant to bring along family members, bring an audiotape recorder to your office. For auditory learners, or those with visual impairments, audiotape recordings can help with remembering instructions. They can also be used to inform relatives and caregivers about treatments or lifestyle changes. The audiotape need only be used for the part of the office visit where directions are being given to the patient.

Research Base: Self-directed Learning, p. 70; Request for Memory Prompts, p. 75

4. **Help the patient to set up an appointment/medication reminder system that works for him or her.**

Work with relatives and caregivers of the older adult patient to set up a reminder system for appointments and medications (times and dosages). If it is not possible to work with relatives, suggest to the patient that he or she subscribe to a telephone reminder service. Information about such services is available from the local Area Agency on Aging. A list of these agencies at the state level is available from the U.S. Administration on Aging's web site: *www.aoa.gov*. A good way to organize medications is the widely used compartmentalized container, where medications are sorted according to days. It is important that the patient knows the importance of keeping this container in the same place in the house.

Research Base: Request for Memory Prompts, p. 75

5. **If email and the World Wide Web are important to your practice, make patients aware of computer training opportunities in your community.**

As more and more practices are availing themselves of the convenience and speed of email and the World Wide Web, many older adult patients may need advice on how to get connected. This can happen through the computer expertise of relatives, but the older adults might want the skills to be able to navigate the Internet themselves. Computer classes are offered in a variety of community settings: senior centers, community colleges, libraries, SeniorNet classes, OASIS centers, CyberSenior.org classes, or adult learning classes through the local school system.

If transmitting messages through email is a part of your practice, your office manager might find it useful to assemble a list of computer training possibilities in your community for distribution to non-computer-literate patients. You may also want to have available for distribution a list of your office's email rules (what is and is not appropriate to communicate via email), the email addresses you want patients to use, and useful and reliable web sites (see page 87 for a suggested list).

Research Base: Distrust/Dislike of Communications Technologies, p. 81

Checklist: At the Office, Before the Consultation

At the Office, Before the Consultation

1. **Provide new patients with welcoming letter that describes a typical office visit (what to expect, how long it might take).**

2. **Train office staff to encourage the patient to ask questions before, during, and after the consultation.**

3. **Set up a waiting room library with age-appropriate health resources and reference materials.**

4. **If possible, have waiting patients review health education materials for their usefulness and readability.**

Details on Checklist Items

1. **Provide new patients with welcoming letter that describes a typical office visit (what to expect, how long it might take).**

A welcoming letter given to a new older adult patient will help him or her to meet the upcoming consultation with an informed mind and less stress about the unknown. Because of differences among practices, the patient's expectations might differ from what is actually going to happen during the consultation. A welcoming letter can also give the patient the opportunity to focus on important issues and to write down questions to discuss with the practitioner.

Important points to cover in such a letter can include the following:

- Statement of welcome to the practice

- Briefly stated philosophy of the practice

- Description of a typical office visit (patient gets weighed, blood pressure and pulse are taken and recorded, chart is updated by assistant, reason for the visit is ascertained, chart is reviewed, discussion of patient's symptoms/condition takes place, examination is done, additional discussion and questions transpire, plans for treatment and follow-up are discussed, prescriptions are renewed/issued, etc.).

- Time typical visit takes

- Follow-up procedures used in the practice

- Important contact information

- What cost/insurance considerations are involved

Research Base: A Focus on the Issues, p. 69; Secure Learning Environment, p. 84

2. **Train office staff to encourage the patient to ask questions before, during, and after the consultation.**

Let patients know, either before they come to the office for a consultation or when they arrive, that you and your office staff are willing and prepared to answer their questions. If you let your older adult patients know in advance that their questions are welcome, you can then advise them to write these questions down, prioritize them, and bring them to

Communicating With Older Adults

the office. There may only be enough time during the consultation for the most important items, so these should be first on the list.

Office staff can also take advantage of the time a new patient spends in the waiting room by introducing the patient to the staff, and orienting the patient to the office set-up (bathrooms, educational literature).

Research Base: Reluctance to Ask Too Many Questions, p. 78

3. **Set up a waiting room library/information center with age-appropriate health resources and reference materials.**

   Have reliable, clearly written reference materials available in your waiting room, and encourage your older adult patients to use these. These can include patient handouts, printouts from reliable web sites, reference books, pamphlets, posters, fact sheets, short videos and other resources. Clear and accurate illustrations and diagrams are particularly useful in helping patients understand what is going on inside their bodies.

   You may also want to consider choosing materials that show older adults engaged in healthy lifestyle practices. Your patients will be more ready to learn new information about their lifestyles, conditions, or medications if they feel that the information is appropriate and realistic for their age group.

   Many of the federal government agencies that are concerned with healthy lifestyles have free materials available (either through the mail or web sites) that are well-suited for older adults.

   These organizations include the following:

   - National Institutes of Health (*www.nih.gov*); particularly the AgePages created by the National Institute on Aging

- Centers for Disease Control and Prevention (*www.cdc.gov*)

- Administration on Aging (*www.aoa.gov*)

- U.S. Department of Health and Human Services (*www.hhs.gov*)

- U.S. Food and Drug Administration (*www.fda.gov*)

- U.S. Department of Agriculture (*www.usda.gov*)

More organizations are listed in the Resources section of this guide beginning at page 87.

A new trend in some physicians' offices is to have a computer-based information kiosk. Patients can access reliable information about their health via CD-ROMs.

Research Base: Use of Appropriate Examples in Aiding Learning, p. 85; Need for Facts to Support Treatments, p. 76

4. **If possible, have waiting patients review health education materials for their usefulness and readability.**

Make sure that any health education materials that you provide to your older adult patients are clear, logical, and easy to see. Test sample materials with older adult patient volunteers to make sure that the materials suit the readership. Some of your office staff can be responsible for managing this review when patients are in the waiting room. A copy of a sample review form is included on page 52.

Research Base: Desire for Appropriate and Easily Understood Information on Lifestyle Changes or Treatments, p. 79

Checklist: Beginning the Consultation

Beginning the Consultation

1. Be alert to the messages you send via your body language and facial expressions.

2. Take steps to avoid appearing rushed and distracted.

3. Ask the patient to state the purpose of the visit and to ask his or her most important questions first.

4. Use the BATHE technique, if appropriate, to find out more about your patient's situation.

Details on Checklist Items

1. Be alert to the messages you send via your body language and facial expressions.

To facilitate learning and a sense of ease in your patients, you need to come across as being open and willing to discuss their questions and concerns. Greet the patient by name when you enter the consulting room, and shake the patient's hand. When talking to the patient, be sure to do the following:

- Face him or her, not a computer screen or the patient's chart

- Keep a pleasant and cheerful demeanor

- Maintain good eye contact

- Sit or stand so that your eyes are on the same level as the patient's

- Avoid crossing your arms, as this can indicate to the patient that you are putting up barriers

- Nod when you understand what the patient is telling you

Research Base: Use of Body Language/Facial Expressions in Indicating Understanding, p. 77

2. Take steps to avoid appearing rushed and distracted.

Make sure that the patient doesn't feel rushed during the consultation. Avoid giving signs of impatience or distraction such as these:

- Answering non-urgent telephone and pager calls
- Writing frantically in the chart
- Looking at your watch
- Keeping one hand on the doorknob of the consulting room
- Working on the computer
- Avoiding eye contact

Some practitioners find it useful to let patients know at the beginning of the consultation that the appointment will be X minutes. In this way, patients don't feel that they are being shortchanged. This is particularly reassuring to older adults who have made an enormous effort to get to the office on time (dressing, arranging transportation, coordinating with relatives). Another strategy to alleviate patient anxiety is to let the patient know when, during the consultation, you have scheduled time for discussion and questions.

Research Base: Secure Learning Environment, p. 84

3. Ask the patient to state the purpose of the visit and to ask his or her most important questions first.

After greeting the patient, ask him or her to state the purpose of the visit: "Why have you come to see me today?" Make a note of this, then give the patient the opportunity to ask any particularly important questions: "Do you have any particular questions or concerns that we should focus on today? Let's just take some time now and get your most important questions on the table."

This strategy gives a patient who has prepared for the visit by making a list of his questions, the chance to share these with you. Make a note of any important points, then revisit these at the end of the consultation.

Research Base: A Focus on the Issues, p. 69

4. Use the BATHE technique, if appropriate, to find out more about your patient's situation.

One of the best ways of establishing a comfortable atmosphere during an office visit is to ask the patient about himself or herself. There is a structured interview technique called BATHE that you may find very useful. It consists of the following steps:

1. **B**ackground ("Tell me what has been happening.")

2. **A**ffect ("How do you feel about that?")

3. **T**rouble ("What's upsetting you most about it?")

4. **H**andling ("How are you handling the situation?")

5. **E**mpathy ("That must have been difficult.")

This technique can quickly bring to light any concerns of the patient that may have an impact on his or her mental and/or physical health. It also fosters a personal connection between the practitioner and the patient, thus creating an atmosphere of trust. The technique is also good for patients who have not prepared a list of questions prior to the visit.

You may think that this technique might take up too much time. However, the technique can bring to light a significant problem much earlier in the consultation than it might otherwise occur.

NOTE: *See the Bibliography for the reference on the BATHE technique.*

Research Base: Secure Learning Environment, p. 84

Checklist: Continuing the Consultation

Continuing the Consultation

1. Be alert to your patient's body language throughout the consultation.

2. Explain the reasons behind your treatment to increase the comfort level of your patient.

3. Avoid using overly technical terms in your explanations.

4. Let your patients know about appropriate and available treatment options.

5. Provide hands-on training for any new skill or piece of equipment that is part of the patient's care.

6. Be sure to discuss medications as part of the visit.

Details on Checklist Items

1. **Be alert to your patient's body language throughout the consultation.**

   If your patient avoids eye contact or has crossed arms, a wrinkled brow, a frown, or other negative signs, it may mean that he or she is confused about the information you are giving, but hesitant to ask questions or otherwise "bother" you. It may also mean that the patient doesn't agree with you, or is suffering from a form of depression. Another point to consider is the cultural orientation of the patient. In some cultures, it is considered impolite to make direct eye contact.

   When you detect these signs, it is important to ask the patient directly, "Am I explaining this clearly enough, or would you like more information? Would a diagram help?" Or you may want to say, "You look like you have a question or concern about what I'm saying. What is it? How can I help?"

   Research Base: Use of Body Language/Facial Expressions in Indicating Understanding, p. 77

2. Explain the reasons behind your treatment to increase the comfort level of your patient.

Provide reliable third-party validation of information so that the older adult increases his or her comfort level with the information you are imparting. These validation sources could include other health care professionals; accurate books, tapes, brochures or web sites; or even toll-free help lines.

Caution the older adult against relying on the opinions of untrained individuals in validating health information. Some web sites and other sources of information may also be inaccurate. Invite questions about any doubts they may have, as well as conflicting information they may find.

Take time to explain, briefly and simply, the science behind your decisions. For example, if you prescribe a new medication, tell your patient what effect the medication has on his or her body (e.g., opens blood vessels), and how it can help the condition or disease (e.g., reduces blood pressure). When possible, refer to the specific symptoms a patient has described and explain how the treatment can control or eliminate them. Write down any significant side effects the medication might have, and advise the patient to call the office if there are any problems with the medication.

Be sure to explain the causes of their conditions, as well as the effects of treatments and lifestyle changes on those conditions. It is important to discuss risk factors and to stress that it is never too late to garner positive effects from lifestyle changes (e.g., quitting smoking, losing excess weight). This discussion will increase the likelihood that the patient will be compliant with a treatment or a change in lifestyle, particularly if you map out the long-term effects if the patient is NOT compliant with the recommendations (diabetic coma if insulin isn't taken, heart disease with a high fat diet, lung cancer with smoking, etc.).

*Research Base: Reliance on Third-Party Valida-
tion, p. 72; Need for Facts to Support Treatment,
p. 76; Role of Cause and Effect in Learning, p. 86*

3. **Avoid using overly technical terms in your explanations.**

   One suggestion is to ask a knowledgeable member of your staff to sit in on some consultations with older adult patients or clients and give you feedback later. Such feedback can include the number of technical terms you used in a session, the observer's perception of the older adults' apparent level of understanding and body language, and whether or not you explained, in a clear and understandable manner, any terms that were questioned by the patient.

   Research Base: Avoiding Overly Technical Terms, p. 83

4. **Let your patients know about appropriate and available treatment options.**

   While Medicare and private insurance may cover most of the costs of a treatment, the co-pay that is required by many insurance companies can be outside the financial resources of people on fixed incomes. Suggest to patients that they check with their insurance companies and with Medicare to find out exactly what treatment options are covered in their cases, and to what extent. If patients (or their caregivers or adult children) have access to the Internet, they can find information about Medicare on *www.medicare.gov*. They may also want to contact their local Area Agency on Aging (AAA) to get help and advice about insurance and Medicare. Information and Referral/Assistance Specialists at the AAAs are skilled in helping in this area. Contact information for local AAAs is in the government pages of the telephone book. Contact information for state AAAs is on the web site of the U.S. Administration on Aging: *www.aoa.gov*. Also suggest to patients that they get a second opinion, if they are interested in exploring treatment options relevant to their cases.

Research Base: Desire to Understand All the Options and Alternatives, p. 80

5. **Provide hands-on training for any new skill or piece of equipment that is part of the patient's care.**

If an older adult patient or client needs to learn a new procedure or how to operate a new device as part of his or her care, it is important to use a hands-on approach to teach that new skill or procedure. This will mean that you will need to have the actual equipment the older adult will be using in your office, or will need to arrange for the older adult to bring the device to your office as part of the consultation. Such training sessions could include the following:

- Injecting insulin
- Conducting a blood sugar test with a kit
- Using a urine test strip
- Managing a colostomy appliance
- Taking blood pressure using a digital device
- Performing a particular exercise
- Using an electric toothbrush or water pick

Include a family member or friend as part of a hands-on instructional session. This provides the older adult with a backup system in case he or she is still unsure about the procedure after leaving your office. (Visiting nurses can also provide supervised training support, as can patient education departments.) Provide written directions that support the hands-on experience and refer to these during the training.

Also, if possible, make suggestions on how to make a piece of equipment fit a patient's abilities better. An example from dentistry would be to adapt a tooth-brush to a patient with arthritis by giving the brush a longer handle or a thicker gripping surface.

Research Base: Chance to Practice and Review, p. 73; Desire for Hands-On Learning, p. 74

6. **Be sure to discuss medications as part of the visit.**

   Since many older adults take more than one medication, it is important to include medications as part of the discussion during the consultation. This is particularly important since interactions between medications can be the very cause of the symptoms the patient has come to see you about. A reluctance to ask too many questions about medications (seeming to "challenge the physician's expertise") can keep problems with medications from coming to light.

   At the end of the discussion, ask the patient if he or she needs any medication refills.

   Research Base: Reluctance to Ask Too Many Questions, p. 78

Checklist: Ending the Consultation

Ending the Consultation

1. **Review any important points arising from the consultation.**

2. **At the end of the visit, provide clear instructions and other information in writing for the patient.**

3. **Provide additional follow-up information such as lifestyle guidelines, treatment options, and the Internet addresses of reliable health web sites.**

Details on Checklist Items

1. **Review any important points arising from the consultation.**

   At the end of the visit, return to the list of questions/ key points that you have noted on the patient's arrival. Be sure that all of the important points have been dealt with and that the patient is satisfied with your explanations.

   Research Base: Chance to Practice and Review, p. 73; Opportunity for Reflection, p. 82

2. **At the end of the visit, provide clear instructions and other information in writing for the patient.**

   Provide older adult patients with a written version (even if it is just notes) of important information, so that they can review it later, assimilate it, and ask questions. Explain any points or terms that are still unclear.

   Make sure to set up a time for the patient to call or visit later, after he or she has had time to think, ask questions, and do some research. These calls may be able to be handled by other health care professionals in the office.

   Research Base: Avoiding Overly Technical Terms, p. 83; Opportunity for Reflection, p. 82

3. **Provide additional follow-up information such as lifestyle guidelines, treatment options, and the Internet addresses of reliable health web sites.**

   Older adults with a health problem want to know what they have to do to fix the problem in the most expeditious way. If this means a change in diet or an exercise program, they need printed guidelines that provide easy-to-understand advice in these areas. Many government-sponsored web sites, as well as those developed by well-respected nonprofit organizations, have this information in downloadable form. One particularly useful guide is Exercise: A Guide from the National Institute on Aging (NIA) at the NIH (Publication Number NIH 99-4258). The guide, available in both English and Spanish, contains information on exercises, motivation and safety. The address is in the resource section of this guide, as are the addresses for:

- To Your Health! Food Safety for Seniors (U.S. Food and Drug Administration)

- AgePages (National Institute on Aging)

Direct computer-literate patients and/or their caregivers to reliable web sites that have clear information on the older adult's condition or treatment. Reliable web sites, such as those sponsored by federal and state government health agencies, can provide ways of assisting older adult patients. They can enlarge the font size on a web site if they have vision problems; view clear illustrations; print out pages; and even find out about, and join, support groups.

Older adults may also be able to find out about clinical trials related to their diseases or conditions. The central government web site for clinical trials is *www.clinicaltrials.gov.*

Research Base: A Focus on the Issues, p. 69; Self-Directed Learning, p. 70

What's Your Opinion?

Title of the Health Education Document:_____

Your Age:_____   Sex: M   F (please circle)

Directions: Please look through this health education document and let us know what you think of it. Circle the answer that best reflects your opinion.

1. The document is easy for me to understand.   Y   N

2. I learned useful information from this document.   Y   N

3. The text and illustrations are easy to see.   Y   N

4. I would recommend this document to a friend.   Y   N

Any other comments or suggestions?

_____

_____

_____

_____

_____

_____

_____

Thank you for taking the time to fill in this form.

What Questions Should I Ask About My Health?

1. **Current and new medications** (How much do I take? When do I take it? How much will it cost? What are the side effects? What are the possible interactions? How long should I take it?)

2. **Symptoms** (Is what I'm feeling "normal"? What do my symptoms mean?)

3. **Laboratory tests** (What tests will I need? What are the tests for? Will my insurance cover the cost?)

4. **Diseases** (What do I have? How did I get it? How will you treat it? Is it contagious?)

5. **Treatments** (How will you treat my condition? How long will the treatment take? How likely is the treatment to work? Are there any other options?)

6. **Diet** (What changes do I have to make in my diet? What will happen if I don't make these changes?)

7. **Exercise** (How much exercise should I do? What types of exercise will work for me? What benefits will I get from the exercise?)

8. **Recreational Activities** (What types of recreation can I do? What types of recreation should I avoid, and why?)

What Items Should I Take With Me To My Next Doctor's Appointment?

- Bring medications or a list of your medications with you to office visits.

- Make a list of important questions you want to ask during the visit.

- Record any unusual symptoms you have that you want to discuss.

- Make a note of any important events in your life that might have an effect on your health.

- Bring your insurance information.

- Bring a personal calendar so that you can schedule your next appointment easily.

- Bring a notepad and pen (or even an audiotape recorder) to record important information from the visit.

- Bring along a friend or family member if you think that would be helpful to you during your visit. The accompanying person can always stay outside during private discussions.

- Bring along a copy of your old medical records, if you have these.

II.
RECOMMENDED PRACTICES FOR PHARMACISTS AND PHARMACY STAFF

This section of the guide provides guidance for health care professionals who work in pharmacy settings. The information in this section provides practical suggestions on how to use the findings from research into older adult learning to improve communication with older adult customers.

The goal of this part of the guide is to increase the comfort level of older adult customers with their medications (use, side effects, interactions, etc.) and to promote compliance with medication regimens through education and support.

Checklist: Informational Materials

Informational Materials for Older Adult Customers

1. Provide printed information on medications, medical equipment, and services that is simple, yet complete; easy to see; illustrated (if appropriate), and to the point.

2. Provide older adult customers with explanations of how their medications work, and what will happen in their bodies if they don't comply with their medication regimen.

3. Be sure that older adult customers have printed information on how to access web-based or telephone-based pharmacy services.

4. Provide Internet addresses for reliable web sites with information on medications for web-savvy customers or caregivers of older adults.

5. Provide older adult customers with documentation from the pharmaceutical company that developed their medication(s).

6. If your pharmacy has a video kiosk, make sure that there are a variety of videos that explain conditions common to older adult customers.

Details on Checklist Items

1. **Provide printed information on medications, medical equipment, and services that is simple, yet complete; easy to see; illustrated (if appropriate), and to the point.**

Older adults are very concerned about their medications. Those on fixed incomes are worried about cost. Most are concerned, at some level, about how often and how long to take their medications, as well as side effects and drug interactions. Any printed information on medications that you provide should be simple, yet complete and to the point. If you provide large-type information on medications, make that available to your older adult customers. Have trained staff available to explain any special procedures for auditory learners.

Educational materials on medications are available from pharmaceutical companies, government agencies, manufacturers of health equipment, and non-profit health organizations. You can test the "user-friendliness" and appropriateness of these materials with your older adult customers by asking them for their opinions. A sample one-page survey to analyze informational materials is included in this guide on page 41. If possible, provide older adult customers with illustrated sets of procedures if they are learning a new skill (such as using a digital blood pressure meter or using a pill-splitter). Videos are particularly useful in showing specific procedures.

Research Base: A Focus on the Issues, p. 69; Self-directed Learning, p. 70; Chance to Practice and

Review, p. 73; Request for Memory Prompts, p. 75; Need for Facts to Support Treatments, p. 76; Desire for Appropriate and Easily Understood Information on Lifestyle Changes or Treatment, p. 79; Use of Appropriate Examples in Aiding Learning, p. 85

2. **Provide older adult customers with explanations of how their medications work, and what will happen in their bodies if they don't comply with their medication regimen.**

Have printed materials available on medications and medical equipment that the older adult customer can share with a third party (friend, relative, caregiver). Understanding how and why medications must be taken helps to promote compliance.

In addition, be sure to let your older adult customers know if there are less expensive generic options available for the medications their physicians or dentists prescribe. Provide them with information describing the action of the generic medication, so that they are assured that they are getting the same benefit from the generic medication as the non-generic form.

Research Base: Social Learning Context, p. 71; Desire to Understand all the Options and Alternatives, p. 80; Role of Cause and Effect in Learning, p. 86

3. **Be sure that older adult customers have printed information on how to access web-based or telephone-based pharmacy services.**

If your pharmacy has the capacity for handling prescriptions online or over the telephone, be sure that your older adult customers have printed information on how to access this service. This will help them to save time, avoid transportation problems, and get what they need as rapidly as possible. A "Frequently Asked Questions" format is often useful in communicating information about web-based services in a clear and friendly fashion. If the older adult is unfamiliar with computers, he or she can pass this information on to a caregiver or relative. In addition to a hesitance to use the Internet, some older customers may also have difficulties navigating through an automated telephone system that asks them to make a number of choices before renewing a prescription. As with the Internet, it helps to have clearly written (large font) directions for how to access this service.

Research Base: A Focus on the Issues, p. 69; Distrust/dislike of Communications Technologies, p. 81

4. **Provide Internet addresses for reliable web sites with information on medications for web-savvy customers or caregivers of older adults.**

There are a number of government web sites with reliable health information. A few of these also have detailed information about medications. MEDLINEplus from the National Library of Medicine (*www.medlineplus.gov*) is very easy to use. A button on the home page of this site links users directly to an alphabetical database of drug information. Pharmaceutical companies that manufacture your customers' medicines may provide useful information as well.

Even if the older adult customer himself or herself does not use a computer, the customer may have relatives or a caregiver who does. This third person can look up the information and share it with the older adult. The power to find reliable information about medications can ease concerns the older adult might have about incomplete information. It is important to stress, however, that health information on the web should NEVER replace the interaction between the customer and his or her physician.

Research Base: Self-directed Learning, p. 70; Social Learning Context, p. 71; Reluctance to Ask Too Many Questions, p. 78

5. **Provide older adult customers with documentation from the pharmaceutical company that developed their medication(s).**

Older adults who want third-party validation of their medications often find comfort in having information about the medication directly from the pharmaceutical company that developed it. You may also want to provide your customers with lists of toll-free numbers they can call with specific questions about their medications. Your older adult customers may find this particularly useful with generic medications.

Research Base: Reliance on Third-Party Validation, p. 72

6. **If your pharmacy has a video kiosk, make sure that there are a variety of videos that explain conditions common to older adult customers.**

Information on the following conditions would be useful to show in a video kiosk: arthritis, osteoporosis, diabetes, heart disease, glaucoma, emphysema, and other diseases common to older adult customers. If possible, choose videos that discuss generic options for customers.

Research Base: Need for Facts to Support Treatments, p. 76

Checklist: Face-to-Face Interactions

Face-to-Face Interactions

1. **If possible, demonstrate to your older adult customers how to use a health device purchased at your pharmacy before the customer takes this home.**

2. **Recommend a reminder system for older adult customers who seem to be struggling to remember things.**

3. Pharmacy staff should be careful not to send negative or intimidating messages to older adult customers via body language or tone of voice.

4. Encourage older adult customers to ask questions about their medications, particularly if these are new.

5. If one of your older adult customers looks confused or questioning about how to take a medication or how to use a health device, be sure to repeat the explanation.

Details on Checklist Items

1. If possible, demonstrate to your older adult customers how to use a health device purchased at your pharmacy before the customer takes this home.

   At the very least, be sure that the customer understands any written directions that come with the device before leaving the pharmacy. It is usually a good idea to review the directions with the customer, and give him or her a chance to ask questions. Any videos that come with new pieces of medical equipment are particularly useful.

   Research Base: Desire for Hands-on Learning, p. 74; Chance to Practice and Review, p. 73, Importance of Reinforcement, p. 84

2. Recommend a reminder system for older adult customers who seem to be struggling to remember things.

   If you notice that some of your older adult customers seem to be struggling to remember things during their interactions with you, you might want to recommend that they arrange with a family member or caregiver to remind them about taking medications.

   Those customers with adequate financial resources

might prefer to subscribe to a telephone-based medication reminder service. Information about these services is available from local area agencies on aging. You may also want to consider notifying the customer's physician about the customer's apparent memory deficiency, in case a memory evaluation is appropriate.

Research Base: Request for Memory Prompts, p. 75

3. **Pharmacy staff should be careful not to send negative or intimidating messages to older adult customers via body language or tone of voice.**

Pharmacy staff, particularly those who are on the front lines of dealing with the public, need to be aware of how their body language can send negative or intimidating messages to older adult customers. It is important that staff have an open and friendly demeanor, and that they make eye contact with their customers. This eye contact is important, because older customers with auditory difficulties can more easily lip-read when a speaker is looking directly at them. Staff should also encourage the customers to ask questions, whether they can be answered directly or need to be referred to another qualified health care provider.

Research Base: Use of Body Language/Facial Expressions in Indicating Understanding, p. 77; Secure Learning Environment, p. 84

4. **Encourage older adult customers to ask questions about their medications, particularly if these are new.**

Many pharmacies now make a habit of asking customers who are picking up prescriptions if they have any questions for the pharmacist. While customers may not have questions at the point of pick-up, a number of questions may occur to them later as they read over the directions and other information accompanying the medication.

Make sure that customers know they can call the pharmacy with questions later on. Let them know what information the pharmacist will need from them to answer their questions (prescription number, medication, dosage, doctor's name, etc.).

Your pharmacy might find it useful to prepare a handout with this information for customers and to post it on the pharmacy's web site. The handout may encourage older adult customers to write down their questions before they come to the pharmacy; and to keep a notebook with questions about their medications. If available, provide drug information sheets in large type for customers with limited vision. Be sure to ask your customers if the type is large enough.

For patients with computer knowledge, provide reliable web site addresses that they can use to answer their own questions about medications. Stress that any online information on medications should not take the place of the interaction between the customer and his or her medical advisor.

Research Base: Reluctance to Ask Too Many Questions, p. 78; Opportunity for Reflection, p. 82

5. **If one of your older adult customers looks confused or questioning about how to take a medication or how to use a health device, be sure to repeat the explanation.**

At the end of any explanation given to the older adult customer, ask if all of the terms used were clear. If not, explain these, and provide any supporting print material, if available. Directions and explanations with clearly labeled diagrams are particularly helpful.

One way to help ensure that customers understand the information about their medications is to establish a customer service policy that includes having the pharmacy technician open the printed drug information that accompanies the medication. He or she can then read about what the drug does, its name, side effects, and how to take it. Usually, those facts are listed and are easy to find on the sheet. While this may take a little more time, in the long run, it may help the customer to feel more comfortable about asking questions and about referring to the printed material at home.

Research Base: Avoiding Overly Technical Terms, p. 83; Secure Learning Environment, p. 84; Importance of Reinforcement, p. 84

What's Your Opinion?

Title of the Health Education Document:_____

Your Age:_____   Sex: M   F (please circle)

Directions: Please look through this health education document and let us know what you think of it. Circle the answer that best reflects your opinion.

1. The document is easy for me to understand.   Y   N

2. I learned useful information from this document.   Y   N

3. The text and illustrations are easy to see.   Y   N

4. I would recommend this document to a friend.   Y   N

Any other comments or suggestions?

_____

_____

_____

_____

_____

_____

Thank you for taking the time to fill in this form.

III.
RECOMMENDED PRACTICES FOR LONG TERM CARE AND ASSISTED LIVING PROVIDERS

This section of the guide provides guidance for health care professionals who work in assisted living communities, sub-acute and rehab care facilities, and skilled nursing facilities. The information in this section provides practical suggestions for improving communication with patients and residents by using research into older adult learning. The findings and recommendations discussed in this section apply only to patients and residents who are able to understand and discuss their own care needs and options and is not intended to apply to communications with those who are suffering from Alzheimer's disease or another form of dementia.

The goal of this part of the guide is to maximize communication with residents to make them feel: comfortable and accepted; as independent as their conditions permit; and confident that they are receiving appropriate care, advice and information about their health.

Checklist: Informational Materials

Informational Materials for Residents

1. Provide clear, accurate, and age-appropriate health information in a variety of formats, in a central location, for residents to use.

2. Post reminders for residents about how to use particular assistive devices, and about health and safety procedures.

3. Post a list of reliable health web site addresses for residents who are computer-literate.

4. Make sure residents have guidance and/or training on how to find reliable health web sites.

Details on Checklist Items

1. Provide clear, accurate, and age-appropriate health information in a variety of formats, in a central location, for residents to use.

Provide brochures, videos, posters, audiotapes, books and other materials that deal with health topics relevant to an older adult audience. It is important to place posters where residents can see them (height is a factor here for residents in wheelchairs). Another option is to set aside a part of the facility with information on health. This could be in a common area, if space permits, or even a bulletin board with posters and brochures on health.

The materials provided need to be clearly written for a lay audience, and preferably well-illustrated. Type size and graphics should be large enough to be seen easily. The tone of the language should be friendly and respectful. The topics should be appropriate for older adults, and the illustrations should reflect the readership of the materials.

Many of the federal government health agencies have free materials available (either through the mail or web sites) that are well-suited for older adults. These organizations include the National Institutes of Health (particularly the AgePages and *Exercise* guide developed by the National Institute on Aging), the Centers for Disease Control and Prevention, the Administration on Aging, the U.S. Department of Health and Human Services, the Food and Drug Administration, the U.S. Department of Agriculture, and many more (listed in the Resource section of this guide.)

Other organizations with clear, easy-to-follow materials on lifestyle regimens include large nonprofit health organizations with long-standing reputations for reliability of content. A few examples are the American Heart Association, the American Cancer Society, the American Lung Association, the American Dental Association, and the American Diabetes Association. Many of these organizations offer patient handouts that can be printed from their web sites.

Research Base: Self-directed Learning, p. 70; Reliance on Third-Party Validation, p. 72; Avoiding Overly Technical Terms, p. 83; Use of Appropriate Examples in Aiding Learning, p. 85

2. **Post reminders for residents about how to use particular assistive devices and about health and safety procedures.**

   If residents feel inclined and are able, they may work together as a group to make reminder posters for different situations. Making the poster can act as a reminder in itself. It is important to change the posters often to maintain interest.

   Research Base: Request for Memory Prompts, p. 75

3. **Post a list of reliable health web site addresses for residents who are computer-literate.**

   If your facility has computers for residents to use, you may want to post a list of reliable health web site addresses. Web sites such as MEDLINEplus (*www.medlineplus.gov*) from the National Library of Medicine and Healthfinder (*www.healthfinder.gov*) from the Department of Health and Human Services have easy-to-find health information. Bookmarking these sites on the facility's computer simplifies the process for residents. You can also refer residents to the SPRY Foundation web site (*www.spry.org*) for an online guide to help older adults find reliable health web sites.

Research Base: Need for Facts to Support Treatments, p. 76; Desire to Understand All the Options and Alternatives, p. 80

4. **Make sure residents have guidance and/or training on how to find reliable health web sites.**

If your facility has computers available for residents to use, you might need to provide training for some of the residents before they feel comfortable using email or searching the web for health information. You might be able to get local middle or high school students to help in this endeavor, since many school systems require their students to perform community service as part of their graduation requirements. You may also be able to arrange for computer-literate, physically able residents or family members to act as peer tutors for residents who want to learn how to use the computer.

Research Base: Distrust/Dislike of Communications Technologies, p. 81

Checklist: Working One-on-One with Residents

Working One-on-One with Residents

1. Advise residents to keep a pad and pen handy to write down questions and concerns.

2. Be aware that just telling someone about health information may not be enough.

3. Use a hands-on approach to show residents how to perform certain procedures.

4. Make sure that medications are clearly visible and sorted into dated containers.

5. Be aware of the role of body language when you communicate.

6. Make sure residents have time to process what you are saying before you move on to a new topic.

7. Be aware of sensory deficits (vision and hearing) and make any necessary adjustments to your communication style.

8. In discussing health care with residents, make sure that they understand why it is important for them to comply with a regimen.

Details on Checklist Items

1. **Advise residents to keep a pad and pen handy to write down questions and concerns.**

   Having a pad and pen (or a clipboard with pen attached) available to use will remind residents to write down questions or concerns as they arise. This will save time in responding to a resident's needs. It is also very useful for patients suffering from memory disorders.

   Research Base: Request for Memory Prompts, p. 75

2. **Be aware that just telling someone about health information may not be enough.**

   Demonstrate any procedures and follow up with written directions. Make sure the print is large enough to be seen by residents with visual impairments. Use pictures and generally accepted symbols to illustrate directions and procedures. Test these with residents to make sure that they are clear and easy to follow. Give the resident time to practice any new procedures with you.

   Research Base: Self-Directed Learning, p. 70

3. **Use a hands-on approach to show residents how to perform certain procedures.**

   Procedures that residents might need a hands-on approach to learn can include the following:

   • Using assistive devices

   • Bathing

- Dressing
- Diabetic care: insulin administration and/or blood glucose check

Ask the resident to demonstrate his or her understanding of the procedure to you several times. If possible, include a family member in the training so as to have a back-up if the resident will be using this procedure outside your facility. Provide large-type (at least 12-point font) written directions (including diagrams, if possible) as reinforcement for the procedure.

Research Base: Desire for Hands-On Learning, p. 74

4. Make sure that medications are clearly visible and sorted into dated containers.

You might suggest to residents that they leave the lid open on the boxes in a medicine sorter once they have taken the medicine for that day.

Research Base: Request for Memory Prompts, p. 75

5. Be aware of the role of body language when you communicate.

If residents appear confused, or are frowning, ask them if they understand what you are saying, or how you can explain it more clearly. (Of course, part of the difficulty may be a hearing disability or over-medication rather than lack of comprehension. The resident may also be suffering from depression, which can account for negative body language.)

Your own body language sends an important message to your residents when you are trying to communicate information about their health. If you are showing them a health-related task (such as taking a new medication or doing a monitoring test) and you appear rushed or impatient, your resident may be distracted by your attitude and not absorb what you are trying to illustrate or demonstrate.

Research Base: Use of Body Language/Facial Expressions in Indicating Understanding, p. 77

6. **Make sure residents have time to process what you are saying before you move on to a new topic.**

   Ask residents to repeat what you said, so you can ensure that they understand what you have told them. You may want to reinforce important information (new health regimen, new directions for medications, diet changes) by writing it down for the resident to use as reference. If you do this, make sure that your writing is large and clear and in the language your resident speaks. The next time you visit the resident, review the new information.

   Research Base: Importance of Reinforcement, p. 84

7. **Be aware of sensory deficits (vision and hearing) and make any necessary adjustments to your communication style.**

   It is extremely important to know your residents and their physical and mental capacities. What appears to be a lack of understanding on the part of the resident, may actually be an inability to hear what you have said or to see instructions that you have written. Make sure that the resident is wearing his or her glasses or hearing aid (turned on) when you are communicating important information. Also check to see if residents who wear dentures have their teeth in when you need to discuss something with them.

   Research Base: Use of Body Language/Facial Expressions in Indicating Understanding, p. 77

8. **In discussing health care with residents, make sure that they understand why it is important for them to comply with a regimen.**

   For example, let residents know what the specific effects on their bodies will be if they take their medications and follow their health regimens. Stress that it is never too late to have positive health effects from sticking to a good diet, exercising, and taking medications properly.

It may be useful to select some residents who are benefiting from following good health practices, and ask them to act as mentors to those who are struggling with adhering to their health plan. Such a "buddy system" can also help older adults who are feeling isolated and on the border of depression.

Research Base: Role of Cause and Effect in Learning, p. 86

Checklist: Working with Residents and Health Care Professionals

Working With Residents and Health Care Professionals

1. **During meetings of residents, ask a health professional to talk about topics of common concern.**

2. **Help prepare residents who are expecting a visit by a health care professional.**

3. **Encourage health care professionals who visit your facility to get to know residents personally.**

4. **If appropriate, arrange visits by health care professionals when family members are available.**

Details on Checklist Items

1. **During meetings of residents, ask a health professional to talk about topics of common concern.**

You can solicit topics from residents in prior meetings or through a communal question box, or give them a list from which to select. Some topics might include the following:

- Benefits of a proper diet

- The importance of adhering to medication schedules

- Safety in the facility and outside

- Benefits of exercise

- New treatments for arthritis

- Dealing with congestive heart failure

- Coping with memory deficits

Let the residents sit in small groups so that they can discuss the topic at hand and ask questions. You may even have residents who are cognitively capable draw up a personal action plan for how they will adhere to a regimen of exercise, diet, and medication.

Research Base: Social Learning Context, p. 71

2. **Help prepare residents who are expecting a visit by a health care professional.**

In helping a resident to prepare for a visit by a health care professional, take the time to interview the him or her about any questions he or she might have for the visitor. Write these down, and have them available when the visitor comes. Encourage the resident to ask a relative to sit in on the visit, if the resident feels that this is appropriate and useful. [See Item 4.]

The resident should be encouraged to ask the health care professional to explain any terms that are unclear. A form that the resident may find useful in preparing for a visit by a health care professional is included in the next section of this guide.

Research Base: A Focus on the Issues, p. 69; Social Learning Context, p. 71; Reluctance to Ask Too Many Questions, p. 78; Avoiding Overly Technical Terms, p. 83

3. **Encourage health care professionals who visit your facility to get to know residents personally.**

Suggest to the healthcare professionals that they keep a brief record of residents' hobbies and details about their families with their health records. A couple of minutes of informal talk relaxes the resident and tends to make him or her more receptive to learning new information such as nutritional advice, medication directions, and lifestyle changes.

It is important that visiting health care professionals talk to residents in areas that are free from such distractions as alarms and intercoms. Meeting areas should also be private to preserve confidentiality between the resident and the health care professional.

Research Base: Secure Learning Environment, p. 84

4. **If appropriate, arrange visits by health care professionals when family members are available.**

Encourage the resident's relatives to assist in collecting information relevant to the resident's questions or concerns during a visit. Any information shared during a visit with the staff of the facility should be done as a joint effort by the resident and the relative. If the relative is willing, he or she can act as a partner with the resident to ensure that the resident's concerns are addressed by the staff of the facility or by the health care professional. Such a partner can also help with reminding the resident about medications, and making sure that the resident gets out to go shopping or for other excursions.

Other relatives might wish to get involved in the care of the resident by reading lifestyle regimen materials to the resident, or converting hard-to-see (but clearly and logically written) educational materials into large posters. These can be displayed in the resident's room or in common areas of the facility. Laminating posters makes them last longer.

Research Base: Social Learning Context, p. 71; Desire for Structured and Easily Understood Protocols for Lifestyle Changes or Treatment, p. 79.

What's Your Opinion?

Title of the Health Education Document:_____

Your Age:_____   Sex: M   F (please circle)

Directions: Please look through this health education document and let us know what you think of it. Circle the answer that best reflects your opinion.

1. The document is easy for me to understand.   Y   N

2. I learned useful information from this document.   Y   N

3. The text and illustrations are easy to see.   Y   N

4. I would recommend this document to a friend.   Y   N

Any other comments or suggestions?

_____

_____

_____

_____

_____

_____

_____

Thank you for taking the time to fill in this form.

What questions should I ask about my health?

1. **Current and new medications** (How much do I take? When do I take it? How much will it cost? What are the side effects? What are the possible interactions? How long should I take it?)

2. **Symptoms** (Is what I'm feeling "normal"? What do my symptoms mean?)

3. **Laboratory tests** (What tests will I need? What are the tests for? Will my insurance cover the cost?)

4. **Diseases** (What do I have? How did I get it? How will you treat it? Is it contagious?)

5. **Treatments** (How will you treat my condition? How long will the treatment take? How likely is the treatment to work? Are there any other options?)

6. **Diet** (What changes do I have to make in my diet? What will happen if I don't make these changes?)

7. **Exercise** (How much exercise should I do? What types of exercise will work for me? What benefits will I get from the exercise?)

8. **Recreational Activities** (What types of recreation can I do? What types of recreation should I avoid, and why?)

IV.
RECOMMENDED PRACTICES FOR SENIOR INFORMATION AND REFERRAL SPECIALISTS

This section of the guide provides guidance for professionals who provide information and referral services to older adults. The information in this section provides practical suggestions for improving communication with clients by using research into older adult learning.

The goal of this part of the guide is to maximize communication with clients to make them feel: comfortable and accepted; as independent as conditions permit; and confident that they are receiving appropriate care, advice and information about their health and other services.

Checklist: Informational Materials

Informational Materials for Clients

1. Provide clear, accurate, and age-appropriate information on health and services in a variety of formats for clients.

2. Make sure that health materials are easy to read and understand.

3. Provide a list of reliable health web site addresses for clients who are computer-literate.

4. Advise clients about where they can get free or inexpensive training to find reliable health web sites.

5. Provide clients with step-by-step guidelines, illustrated, if possible, on how to follow a health regimen.

6. **Let clients know where they can find reliable information on medications.**

7. **Provide, or help the client develop, a large-print list of important telephone numbers.**

Details on Checklist Items

1. **Provide clear, accurate, and age-appropriate information on health and services in a variety of formats for clients.**

   Provide brochures, videos, posters, audiotapes, books and other materials that deal with health and services relevant to an older adult audience. Many of the federal government health agencies have free materials available (either through the mail or web sites) that are well suited for older adults. These organizations include the National Institutes of Health (particularly the AgePages and *Exercise* guide developed by the National Institute on Aging), the Centers for Disease Control and Prevention, the Administration on Aging, the U.S. Department of Health and Human Services, the Food and Drug Administration, the U.S. Department of Agriculture, and many more (listed in the Resource section of this guide.)

   Other organizations with clear, easy-to-follow materials on lifestyle regimens include large nonprofit health organizations with long-standing reputations for reliability of content. A few examples are the American Heart Association, the American Cancer Society, the American Lung Association, the American Dental Association, and the American Diabetes Association. Many of these organizations offer handouts that can be printed from their web sites.

   Research Base: Self-directed Learning, p. 70; Reliance on Third-Party Validation, p. 72; Avoiding Overly Technical Terms, p. 83; Use of Appropriate Examples in Aiding Learning, p. 85

2. **Make sure that health materials are easy to read and understand.**

The materials provided need to be clearly written for a lay audience, and preferably well illustrated. Type size and graphics should be large enough to be seen easily. The tone of the language should be friendly and respectful. The topics should be appropriate for older adults, and the illustrations should reflect the readership of the materials.

Research Base: Use of Appropriate Examples in Aiding Learning, p. 85

3. **Provide a list of reliable health web site addresses for clients who are computer-literate.**

If your client owns and knows how to use a computer, you may want to provide a list of reliable health web site addresses. Web sites such as MEDLINEplus (*www.medlineplus.gov*) from the National Library of Medicine and Healthfinder (*www.healthfinder.gov*) from the Department of Health and Human Services have easy-to-find health information. Bookmarking these sites on the client's computer simplifies the process for later use. You can also refer clients to the SPRY Foundation web site (*www.spry.org*) for an online guide to help older adults find reliable health web sites.

Research Base: Need for Facts to Support Treatments, p. 76; Desire to Understand All the Options and Alternatives, p. 80

4. **Advise clients about where they can get free or inexpensive training to find reliable health web sites.**

If your client does not know how to use a computer, you might need to provide information on training resources. You might be able to get local middle or high school students to help in this endeavor, since many school systems require their students to perform community service as part of their graduation requirements. You may also be able to arrange for computer-literate, physically able older adults in the community, or family members, to act as peer tutors for clients who want to learn how to use the computer.

Research Base: Distrust/Dislike of Communications Technologies, p. 81

5. **Provide clients with step-by-step guidelines, illustrated, if possible, on how to follow a health regimen.**

Older adults with a health problem want to know what they have to do to fix the problem in the most expeditious way. If this means a change in diet or an exercise program, they need printed guidelines that provide easy-to-understand advice in these areas. Many government-sponsored web sites, as well as those developed by well-respected nonprofit organizations, have this information in downloadable form. One particularly useful guide is *Exercise: A Guide from the National Institute on Aging* (NIA) at the NIH (Publication Number NIH 99-4258). The guide, available in both English and Spanish, contains information on exercises, motivation and safety. The address is in the resource section of this guide, as are the addresses for:

- To Your Health! Food Safety for Seniors (U.S. Food and Drug Administration)

- AgePages (National Institute on Aging)

Direct computer-literate clients and/or their caregivers to reliable web sites that have clear information on the older adult's condition or treatment. Reliable web sites, such as those sponsored by federal and state government health agencies, can provide ways of assisting older adults. They can enlarge the font size on a web site if they have vision problems; view clear illustrations; print out pages; and even find out about, and join, support groups.

Research Base: A Focus on the Issues, p. 69; Self-Directed Learning, p. 69

6. **Let clients know where they can find reliable information on medications.**

   Government health web sites are among the most reliable and accurate sources of information about medications. Some of the easiest to navigate are:

   - Medlineplus (*www.medlineplus.gov*), the consumer web site from the National Library of Medicine

   - Healthfinder (*www.healthfinder.gov*), the health web site from the U. S. Department of Health and Human Services

   - High Blood Pressure web page from the National Heart, Lung, and Blood Institute (*www.nhlbi.nih.gov/hbp/index.html*)

   For those without Internet access or skills, the Merck Index is an excellent source of information on medications.

   Research Base: Need for Facts to Support Treatments, p. 76

7. **Provide, or help the client develop, a large-print list of important telephone numbers.**

   One resource that you can help your client develop is a list, in large print, of important telephone numbers. These can include:

   - Physician

   - Hospital emergency room

   - Poison Control Center

   - Nearby relatives and neighbors

   - Pharmacy

   - Insurance company

- Transportation services
- Area Agency on Aging
- Medicare (1-800-MEDICARE or 1-800-633-4227)
- Social Security Administration (1-800-772-1213)

If this list is laminated, it will last a long time and be water-resistant. Multiple copies are also a good idea. Convenient places to post such lists are on the refrigerator, on a kitchen cupboard door, by the telephone, by the bedside telephone, or on a kitchen bulletin board.

Research Base: Request for Memory Prompts, p. 75

Checklist: Working One-on-One with Clients

Working One-on-One with Clients

1. Be aware that just telling someone about health and services may not be enough.

2. Ask about the most important questions or needs the client has early in the visit, so that these don't get forgotten.

3. Use a hands-on approach to show clients how to perform tasks or procedures.

4. Be aware of the role of body language when you communicate.

5. Make sure clients have time to process what you are saying before you move on to a new topic.

6. Be aware of sensory deficits (vision and hearing) and make any necessary adjustments to your communication style.

7. Review important points at the end of the visit.

8. Provide follow-up resources for questions that arise after you have ended the visit.

Details on Checklist Items

1. **Be aware that just telling someone about health and services may not be enough.**

   Explain the information that the client needs to know and follow this up with a written version. Make sure the print is large enough to be seen by clients with visual impairments. Use pictures and generally accepted symbols to illustrate directions and procedures. Test these with your client base to make sure that they are clear and easy to follow. Give the client time to practice any new procedures with you.

   Research Base: Self-Directed Learning, p. 70; Chance to Practice and Review, p. 73.

2. **Ask about the most important questions or needs the client has early in the visit, so that these don't get forgotten.**

   When you set up an appointment with a client, ask the client to write down (if possible) the most important points you need to cover on your visit. If the client has difficulty writing, ask that a family member or caregiver write down the client's questions or concerns so that you don't miss dealing with any issues when you do make your visit.

   When you begin your visit, ask to see the list of important questions first, and deal with these right away. When appropriate, write down your responses to these questions (in large, clear writing), so that the client can share these with family members and refer to them later on.

   Research Base: Request for Memory Prompts, p. 75

3. **Use a hands-on approach to show clients how to perform tasks or procedures.**

   Procedures that clients might need a hands-on approach to learn can include the following:

- Using assistive devices
- Using health monitoring devices

Ask the client to demonstrate his or her understanding of the procedure to you several times. If possible, include a family member in the training so as to have a back-up for the client. Provide large-type (at least 12-point font) written directions (including diagrams, if possible) as reinforcement for the procedure.

Research Base: Desire for Hands-On Learning, p. 74

4. **Be aware of the role of body language when you communicate.**

   If clients appear confused, or are frowning, ask them if they understand what you are saying, or how you can explain it more clearly. (Of course, part of the difficulty may be a hearing disability or over-medication rather than lack of comprehension. The client may also be suffering from depression, which can account for negative body language.)

   Your own body language sends an important message to your clients when you are trying to communicate information. If you are showing them how to perform a task and you appear rushed or impatient, your client may be distracted by your attitude and not absorb what you are trying to illustrate or demonstrate.

   Research Base: Use of Body Language/Facial Expressions in Indicating Understanding, p. 77

5. **Make sure clients have time to process what you are saying before you move on to a new topic.**

   Ask clients to repeat what you said, so you can ensure that they understand what you have told them. You may want to reinforce important information (new schedule for services, for example) by writing it down for the client to use as reference. If you do this, make sure that your writing is large and clear and in the language your client speaks. The next time you visit the client, review the new information.

Research Base: Importance of Reinforcement, p. 84

6. **Be aware of sensory deficits (vision and hearing) and make any necessary adjustments to your communication style.**

As much as possible, it is important to know your clients' physical and mental capacities. What appears to be a lack of understanding on the part of the client may actually be an inability to hear what you have said or to see instructions that you have written. Make sure that the client is wearing his or her glasses or hearing aid (turned on) when you are communicating important information. Check to see that clients who wear dentures have their teeth in when you need to discuss something with them.

Research Base: Use of Body Language/Facial Expressions in Indicating Understanding, p. 77

7. **Review important points at the end of the visit.**

At the end of your visit, review any key points that you have talked about during the visit. Be sure that all of the important points have been covered and that the client is satisfied with the information.

Research Base: Research Base: Chance to Practice and Review, p. 73; Opportunity for Reflection, p. 82

8. **Provide follow-up resources for questions that arise after you have ended the visit.**

Provide clients with a written version (even if it is just notes) of important information, so that they can review it later, assimilate it, and ask questions. Make sure that your writing is large enough to see easily.

Let the client read over your notes before your end your visit. Explain any points or terms that are still unclear.

Make sure to provide the client with information on how to reach you or a colleague, in case he or she thinks of additional questions after your visit.

Research Base: Opportunity for Reflection, p. 82

Checklist: Working with Clients and Health Care Professionals

Working With Clients and Health Care Professionals

1. Help prepare clients who are expecting to visit their health care professional in the near future by writing down one – three of their key questions.

2. Encourage clients to write down and keep their appointments with their health care professionals.

3. Advise clients to contact their health care professional before an office visit, to find out what to bring along (medications, insurance information, Medicare card).

4. Encourage clients to write down key points during a visit to their health care professional, or ask an accompanying relative to do so.

5. Recommend to clients that they follow up with the health care professional if they think of questions later they forgot to ask during the visit.

Details on Checklist Items

1. Help prepare clients who are expecting to visit their health care professional in the near future by writing down one – three of their key questions.

In helping a client prepare for a visit to a health care professional, take the time to interview him or her about any important questions he or she might have. Write these down in large print, and leave them with the client. Encourage the client to ask a relative or friend to come along on the visit, if the client feels that this is appropriate and useful.

The client should be encouraged to ask the health care professional to explain any unclear terms. A form that the client may find useful in preparing for a visit to a health care professional is included in this guide.

Research Base: A Focus on the Issues, p. 69; Reluctance to Ask Too Many Questions, p. 78

2. **Encourage clients to write down and keep their appointments with their health care professionals.**

Work with relatives and caregivers of the older adult client to set up a reminder system for appointments. If it is not possible to work with relatives or friends, suggest to the client that he or she subscribe to a telephone reminder service. This service will call clients to remind them about appointments in enough time to arrange for transportation and other assistance. A number of communities offer telephone reminder services through community volunteers. Other reminder services are available commercially.

Research Base: Request for Memory Prompts, p. 75

3. **Advise clients to contact their health care professional before an office visit, to find out what to bring along (medications, insurance information, Medicare card).**

Encourage the client and/or caregiver to contact the office of the health care professional before a visit to find out what to bring along and how to prepare. This preparation can include:

- Writing down important questions in advance

- Bringing along an insurance or Medicare card

- Bringing in medications

- Inviting a family member or friend to come along on the office visit

- Tracking a symptom and keeping notes on it

- Keeping and bringing in a record of his or her weight

- Keeping and bringing in a record of what he or she typically eats in a day

- Reflecting on recent events in his or her life that might have implications on physical or mental health

- Remembering to bring in old medical records (if a new patient).

Research Base: A Focus on the Issues, p. 69

4. **Encourage clients to write down key points during a visit to their health care professional, or ask an accompanying relative to do so.**

Encourage the client to ask relatives or friends to assist in collecting information relevant to the client's questions or concerns during a visit. If the relative is willing, he or she can act as a partner with the client to ensure that the client's concerns are addressed by the health care professional. Such a partner can also help with reminding the client about medications and appointments.

Other relatives might wish to get involved in the care of the client by reading lifestyle regimen materials to the client, or converting hard-to-see (but clearly and logically written) educational materials into refrigerator or bulletin board posters. Laminating posters makes them last longer and resist water damage.

Research Base: Request for Memory Prompts, p. 75

5. **Recommend to clients that they follow up with the health care professional if they think of questions**

later they forgot to ask during the visit.

Advise the client to follow up after a visit to a health care professional if any points or questions arise after the visit. Many people are under stress during office visits, and need time to think and do some research before they can come up with questions they wish they had asked. The follow-up calls may be able to be handled by other health care professionals in the office.

Research Base: Reluctance to Ask Too Many Questions, p. 78; Opportunity for Reflection, p. 82

Checklist: Talking on the Telephone with Clients

Talking on the Telephone with Clients

1. **Be friendly and welcoming when taking a call from a client.**

2. **Ask for specific questions early in the conversation, and write these down for later review.**

3. **Provide resources that support your information, referrals, and assistance.**

4. **Review key points at the end of the call.**

Details on Checklist Items

1. **Be friendly and welcoming when taking a call from a client.**

A friendly and welcoming tone of voice when taking a call from an older adult client puts that caller at ease and makes him or her more receptive to any information you may impart. Callers who feel that they may be "bothering you" will be less likely to ask all the questions they may need to ask, and will feel dissatisfied at the end of the conversation.

Research Base: Secure Learning Environment, p. 84

2. Ask for specific questions early in the conversation, and write these down for later review.

As some older adult callers may have memory difficulties, be sure to ask very early on in the conversation about any and all questions the caller may have. Make a note of these, and then refer to your notes as the conversation proceeds. You may need to prompt the caller if he or she forgets a question later in the conversation. Review the notes together at the end of the call.

Research Base: Request for Memory Prompts, p. 75

3. Provide resources that support your information, referrals, and assistance.

Older adults with problems want to know what they have to do to fix their problems in the most expeditious way. If this means a change in diet or an exercise program, they need printed guidelines that provide easy-to-understand advice in these areas. Many government-sponsored web sites, as well as those developed by well-respected nonprofit organizations, have this information in downloadable form. One particularly useful guide is *Exercise: A Guide from the National Institute on Aging* (NIA) at the NIH (Publication Number NIH 99-4258). The guide, available in both English and Spanish, contains information on exercises, motivation and safety. The address is in the resource section of this guide, as are the addresses for:

- To Your Health! Food Safety for Seniors (U.S. Food and Drug Administration)

- AgePages (National Institute on Aging)

Direct computer-literate patients and/or their caregivers to reliable web sites that have clear information on the older adult's problem or issue. Reliable web sites, such as those sponsored by federal and state government health agencies, can provide ways of assisting older adult patients. They can enlarge the font size on a web site if they have vision problems; view clear illustrations; print out pages; and even find out about, and join, support groups.

Research Base: A Focus on the Issues, p. 69; Self-Directed Learning, p. 70

4. **Review key points at the end of the call.**

At the end of your call, review any key points that you have discussed. Be sure that all of the important points have been covered and that the caller is satisfied with the information. Also discuss what action will be taken on your end as a result of the call, or what action the caller should take. Verify the caller's contact information for accuracy at the end of the call.

Research Base: Chance to Practice and Review, p. 73; Opportunity for Reflection, p. 82

V.

ACCOMMODATING THE COMMUNICATIONS AND LEARNING NEEDS OF OLDER ADULTS IN A HEALTH CARE SETTING

RESEARCH FINDINGS AND BACKGROUND

This section presents nineteen distinct factors significant in understanding and addressing the communications and learning needs of older adults. All are supported by the research findings of the joint SPRY/Robert Wood Johnson Foundation project: *Bridging Principles of Older Adult Learning.*

Following each learning factor is a brief background discussion explaining why the factor was found to be significant and suggesting a some of the implications for practical application.

Additional resources for further consideration of each of the nineteen learning factors are organized and presented in the second part of this section.

Source citations for the nineteen learning factors are listed in the third part of this section.

Nineteen Older Adult Learning Factors

Section 1
Older Adult Learning Factor: A Focus on the Issues

Many older adults have a tendency to focus on a particular problem or issue. This translates into a desire to solve the problem or address the issue in the most expeditious way, and into a reluctance to consider other issues until the first one is resolved.

Older adults base their learning and decisions on a lifetime of experience, knowledge, and skills. This might mean that they need less basic instruction than younger people in some matters regarding their health. It can also mean, if their existing knowledge base in some areas is flawed or incomplete, they may need to "unlearn" and "relearn" some concepts, which is always a difficult process.

There can be some stumbling blocks in this process of unlearning and relearning. Even though their knowledge may be incomplete, or even incorrect regarding some aspects of their health, some older adults may not wish to spend time on a lengthy educational process. Part of the reason for this tendency is a sense that, since they are in the later years of their lives, their time is precious and not to be wasted. Other reasons may include a reluctance to "bother" the health care professional, or a reluctance to find things out about their condition that they might not want to know. This tendency has implications that require health care professionals to take special steps when communicating information. These include the following:

- Answers to specific health questions that are quick, yet complete.

- Reliable health information in a form that is easy to see and understand.

- Solutions to health problems that detail just what the older adult or caregiver must do to achieve the desired result.

Section 2
Older Adult Learning Factor: Self-directed Learning

Older adults prefer to choose their own method, pace, and form of assistance for learning new information, rather than having these things selected by someone else.

Background

From their long experience in formal and informal educational settings, most older adults have a keen awareness of what they want to learn and how they learn it best. Many older adults have been conditioned to accept information via the spoken or printed word, as that was the normal method of instruction in many schools as they were "learning to learn". Still others process information best when it is accompanied by pictures (either moving or still). The advent of television in the 1950s has "re-conditioned" many older adults to learn more readily from pictorial representations of information than from printed or spoken words. The implications that this has for communicating health information to older adults include the following:

- Older adults want choice in selecting alternative methods of communication available when they are learning health information.

- Older adults want to have control over how they will learn health information.

Section 3
Older Adult Learning Factor: Social Learning Context

Many older adults learn best when they have the opportunity to discuss new information with their peers or family members in a group setting.

Background

Older adult learners want to share their knowledge with others (Gamache, 1997). They also want to appear in control and independent, qualities conducive to a peer teaching and learning approach. While this may not be practical in a typical clinical setting, it may be very useful in community health programs (such as those sponsored by local hospitals), or in settings such as senior centers and long-term care facilities. In all of these settings, older adults have the opportunity to get together in groups and avail themselves of one another's experience and questions. Group settings also allow older adults the opportunity to verbalize what they have learned, giving them a way to process and clarify new information. The implications that this has for communicating health information to older adults include the following:

- Older adults want the opportunity to be able to share new health information with peers and family.

- Older adults benefit by teaching others their newly acquired health information.

- Older adults benefit by verbalizing what they have just learned, for it requires them to process and digest the information.

Section 4
Older Adult Learning Factor: Reliance on Third-Party Validation

Many older adults find new information more reliable if a trusted third party validates this information.

Background

Most older adults will not have biology or health backgrounds. This makes them highly reliant upon the expertise of the health care professional as a source of health information. Third-party validation can help the older adult to feel more confident about the reliability of the health information. The "third party" in this case should be a person or other information source at least as qualified as the health care professional imparting the original information. Third parties can include (depending upon the case) trained health care professionals, highly regarded health or medical reference materials, or reliable web sites (such as those from the National Institutes of Health, the Centers for Disease Control and Prevention, the U.S. Department of Health and Human Services, or other government agencies).

It is important to note that while reliable and accurate third-party validation can increase an older adult's confidence in the health information, the absence of validation by a trusted but untrained person (such as a friend or relative) can have just the opposite effect. If the older adult has more faith in the opinion of the untrained friend or relative than in the trained health care professional, the older adult might disregard facts in favor of incorrect information.

The implications that this has for communicating health information to older adults include the following:

- Older adults may want third-party validation of the health information they are receiving from the health care professional.

- Older adults may not believe accurate information from a trained health care professional if this is not supported by the opinion of a trusted (yet untrained) friend or relative.

Section 5
Older Adult Learning Factor: Chance to Practice and Review

Many older adults learn new procedures best if they have the chance to review and practice them under the guidance of a knowledgeable professional.

Background

Older adults want to have control over their environment so as to maintain their independence as long as possible. But many of them may be experiencing a decline in cognitive capacity (whether real or perceived) and may have some difficulties with memory. One way to reconcile these characteristics is to provide the older adult with an opportunity to practice a new health-related skill (such as a technical procedure or exercise) while in the presence of a knowledgeable health care professional. The older adult will benefit from reviewing new written or oral health information with the health care professional, while practicing a new skill.

One implication that this has for communicating health information to older adults is the following:

- Older adults want to maintain control over their lives while coping with possible reduction in physical and/or mental capacity. Practice of new skills and review of new information can help them to maintain some control.

Section 6
Older Adult Learning Factor: Desire for Hands-On Learning

Many older adults learn new procedures best (especially those involving devices or tools) if they have the opportunity to learn the procedures using the actual devices under the supervision of a professional.

Background

Depending upon their formal educational experiences, many older adults may not have had much hands-on instruction in their lives. Research shows, however, that older adults learn new skills more rapidly and readily if they do have hands-on experience. This is particularly important if the older adult is learning how to use a new medical device or perform a new procedure (take blood pressure, measure blood sugar, change a colostomy bag, use an assistive device, etc.)

One implication that this has for communicating health information to older adults is the following:

- Although older adults may be unfamiliar with learning from a hands-on approach, research supports using hands-on instruction with this age group.

Section 7
Older Adult Learning Factor: Request for Memory Prompts

Many older adults (particularly those with memory deficits) learn new information best when it is accompanied by strategies to prompt their memories. [Note: In many patients with dementia, there will come a time when compensatory strategies no longer work.]

Background

Some older adults experience a decline in memory function as they age. They can benefit greatly by using memory prompts associated with new health information, particularly information that requires a new procedure (taking medications, measuring a vital sign, undergoing therapy, exercising, etc.). The easiest way for many people to remember a procedure is to write it down. This works well if the writer of the information has captured it correctly, and the patient can read it. Those who have problems with English, in addition to memory lapses, will not benefit from directions or procedures written in English. They need directions written in the language they can read, or directions that are illustrated with clear graphics. Some patients benefit by using devices or services such as dated pill keepers, telephone reminder services, index cards with important health information (e.g., medications and dosages), diagrams with instructions, and posted health regimen reminders in large print.

The implications that this has for communicating health information to older adults include the following:

- Older adults with memory deficits benefit by using a variety of reminders to help them comply with health regimens.

- Reminders can be verbal or graphic, according to the literacy and learning styles of the older adult.

Section 8
Older Adult Learning Factor: Need for Facts to Support Treatments

Many older adults learn new information about their conditions and treatments best if it is supported by facts (research findings, basic science, long-established treatment procedures).

Background

Older adults want to maintain control of a learning situation, so as to keep their independence. People differ, of course, but many older patients do not wish to rely completely upon the opinion of their health care professionals, particularly when a health situation is dangerous or difficult to accept. They want the facts from a well-known, reliable source to back up the opinion of the health care professional. The most commonly used form of support for a particular treatment is the second opinion.

Many older adults want to know what the latest research has to say about a particular course of treatment, and what the alternatives are. This is particularly true in the case of cancer patients, who are typically willing to try any treatment that has a chance of working. At the same time, they want to know the side effects of the treatment, as well as how much it might cost.

The Internet has helped to increase knowledge of and interest in clinical trials. Many older adults who would never have considered involving themselves in a clinical trial may now be more willing to do so, since they can find out the details of the trials on the Web. A reliable source such as the government web site *www.clinicaltrials.gov* increases the older adult's confidence in participating in clinical studies.

The implications that this has for communicating health information to older adults include the following:

- Older adults want substantiation for the health information they receive from one source.

- Providing background information and second opinion options to older adult patients and clients increases their confidence in treatment options.

Section 9
Older Adult Learning Factor: Use of Body Language/ Facial Expressions in Indicating Understanding

While not unique to older adults, body language and facial expressions play an important role in indicating whether or not an individual understands new information.

Background

A great deal has already been written on the role of body language in how older adults and health care professionals communicate. This literature, however, tends to focus on how messages are sent and received between the older adult patient and the health care professional, not on how the older adult is learning new information. The health care professional can take cues from the facial expressions and other body language of the older adult in much the same way that classroom teachers do: they watch their students' faces for signs of confusion and of lack of understanding. They also watch for such behaviors as folded arms (reluctance to take in information) or complete lack of eye contact (possible lack of interest or inability to understand what is being said.)

Body language is affected by culture, fitness, age, sex, and many other factors. For example, while good eye contact during discussions between a patient and a health care professional is acceptable in Western cultures, this may not be true for other cultures. Another factor to consider is the physical state of the patient. He or she may be sitting stiffly and looking down in an attempt to control pain - not necessarily because he or she does not understand what the health care professional is saying. The best way to sort out possible mixed messages from body language is to ask the patient directly if he or she understands what you are saying. You may want the patient to paraphrase what you have said.

The implications that this has for communicating health information to older adults include the following:

- Body language is important in gauging whether or not an older adult understands new information or agrees with the practitioner.

- The body language of the person giving the information can send a message to the older adult that he/she is open to receiving questions and giving explanations.

- Body language may mean different things in different cultures and situations.

Section 10
Older Adult Learning Factor: Reluctance to Ask Too Many Questions

Many older adults hesitate to ask questions that may clarify their understanding of a concept because of a fear of appearing uninformed, or a hesitance to "bother" the health care professional. They may not know *what* to ask and *how* to ask it.

Background

The reluctance to ask questions of the health care professional is one of the biggest problems older adult patients have in getting comprehensive treatment. Many older adults hesitate to ask questions of their health care professionals because they don't want to "bother them" or "waste their time." This feeling can be exacerbated by health care professionals who are obviously rushed, who look at their watches constantly during consultations, and who appear to be unwilling to listen to the patient or client.

Communicating With Older Adults

It is important to be aware of any signals that you give to your patients that indicate that their questions are unwelcome, or that you are too rushed to answer any questions. Some of the greatest learning takes place through questioning, because many people do not ask questions unless they have a need to know. Take advantage of these learning moments by encouraging your older adult patients to ask questions during a consultation, or to call the office after the consultation.

The implications that this has for communicating health information to older adults include the following:

- Older adults may be hesitant to ask questions of a busy health care professional.

- Older adults learn a great deal through the questioning process. They should therefore be encouraged to ask questions.

Section 11
Older Adult Learning Factor: Desire for Appropriate and Easily Understood Information on Lifestyle Changes or Treatment

Many older adults learn and comply most easily with new procedures for lifestyle changes and treatments if the new procedures are logically structured, easy to see, and clearly written.

Background

There is a plethora of health materials available for all ages - some clearly and carefully written, and others less so. If you are going to distribute materials to patients or clients about lifestyle changes (how to stop smoking, how to follow a low-fat diet, how to restrict salt intake, etc.), be sure to test these with older adults whose opinions you value. Select materials that are clear and logical. If they are print materials, they should be in large type (font) with high contrast between the objects on the page and the background, so that the information can be seen easily. Similar rules follow for web sites with lifestyle information. The font on the web site should be large enough to be seen easily, and the contrast between the screen text and the background should be very high (black on white or off-white).

The implications that this has for communicating health information to older adults include the following:

- Older adults who are engaged in making lifestyle changes want to have guidance on how to do it.

- Information about lifestyle changes should be clear, logical, and easy to see (high contrast between font and background, lots of white space, large font, clear graphics).

Section 12
Older Adult Learning Factor: Desire to Understand All the Options and Alternatives

Many older adults want to learn about alternative treatments so as to make the choice best suited to their lifestyles and financial means.

Background

In the past, most older adult patients accepted the decisions of their health care professionals without question or challenge. The dawn of the "information age," however, has changed that attitude in many older adults. They are more and more aware of alternative treatment options, through friends, family, the Internet, television, and other forms of media. Since many of them have limited financial resources, they want to know if there are less expensive treatment options available. They may also be looking for treatment options that are more suited to their lifestyles. You can either provide this information for them directly, if you have it, or put them in touch with a resource that has the information (another professional, organization, resource or web site).

The implications that this has for communicating health information to older adults include the following:

- Older adults want to know what choices they have for treatments so as to make the most appropriate decisions for their lifestyles and financial situations.

- Many older adults have changed from being passive recipients of health decisions to being active participants in the information gleaning and assimilating process. This means that they want a variety of informational resources to access before they make health decisions.

Section 13
Older Adult Learning Factor: Distrust/Dislike of Communications Technologies

Some older adults need to overcome a dislike/distrust of communications technologies such as email, voicemail, or the World Wide Web, in order to see these as learning tools.

Background

Since many older adults did not grow up with computer technology as a learning/information tool, they may be hesitant to use this as a means of learning new health information. They might be reluctant, for example, to sign up for a medication reminder service that is online, or to communicate with their doctor's office or pharmacy via email. They may also not have any access to a computer.

They may not have any web searching skills, and so may be frustrated when trying to search the web for reliable health information. A number of older adults rely upon their children and/or caregivers to access health information via the web.

The implications that this has for communicating health information to older adults include the following:

- Many older adults have no computer experience and may not consider computer technology to be a comfortable means of accessing health information.

- Many older adults rely upon their children and/or caregivers to supply them with information via the Internet. These children and caregivers must therefore have reliable sources of information.

Section 14
Older Adult Learning Factor: Opportunity for Reflection

Many older adults learn most readily if given an opportunity to reflect on new information at their own pace, coming back later with questions.

Background

In the typical brief encounters that older adults have with their health professionals, a great deal of information can be transferred. Such information may include a diagnosis, treatment options, recommendations for lifestyle changes, instructions on medications, rules and regulations, insurance information, and much more. People of any age may have difficulty absorbing all this information at once, but for adults with sensory and/or memory impairments, the result can be much worse.

One way of dealing with this concern is to segment the information. Give essentials during a consultation or meeting, accompanied by the information in writing. Follow this by suggesting an opportunity for further interaction via the telephone or on a return visit. This gives the older adult the chance to assimilate the new information, perhaps do some informal research, and then generate questions for the follow-up opportunity.

One implication that this has for communicating health information to older adults is the following:

- Some older adults learn new information most readily if they are able to learn it at their own pace.

This may mean that the information should be given to them in segments, with time for reflection in between.

Section 15
Older Adult Learning Factor: Avoiding Overly Technical Terms

Most older adults will not have a biology or medical background, but will wish to understand their condition and its treatment. They learn best if the language used to explain their condition and/or treatment is free from overly sophisticated terms, jargon, and abbreviations.

Background

There is a difference between using simple, clear language and oversimplifying information to the point of inaccuracy. Professionals have a tendency to use the language of their field, often forgetting that this language is not meaningful to their patients. They might use acronyms and abbreviations that are cryptic to the general public, or explain a situation to a patient or client using extremely technical language. This might be impressive to the client or patient, but doesn't help to promote understanding. The best route to follow in explaining a health situation to an older adult is to use everyday terms (augmented, but not replaced, by the technical terms), diagrams, models, or even videos.

The implications that this has for communicating health information to older adults include the following:

- Older adults without life science backgrounds learn health information most readily if that information is presented in clear, everyday language that avoids overly technical terms or medical jargon.

- Older adults without life science backgrounds benefit by having medical explanations enhanced by graphics, diagrams, or videos.

Section 16
Older Adult Learning Factor: Secure Learning Environment

Most older adults learn new information best in a secure, relaxed environment.

Background

A clinical consultation can be a high-stress situation for many older adults. Such stress reduces the capacity for logical thought and learning. It is up to the practitioner to lessen the potential for stress in these settings by making sure that the patient or client is comfortable, does not feel rushed or embarrassed, and is encouraged to ask questions. Many older adults feel particularly embarrassed about bringing up sensitive issues with their health care professionals, particularly those having to do with incontinence and sexual function.

The implications that this has for communicating health information to older adults include the following:

- Older adults need to be made to feel comfortable when interacting with their health care professionals, so that they are ready to learn the health information they might resist under stress.

- It is up to the health care professional to create a comfortable atmosphere for the older adult, so that the patient feels free to ask questions and request clarification when necessary.

Section 17
Older Adult Learning Factor: Importance of Reinforcement

Many older adults require reassurance that what they have just learned is correct.

Background

After many years of experience with learning and communication, older adults typically do not pretend that they understand something when they don't, unlike many of their younger counterparts. If they are hearing new health information from a health care professional, and they are not sure that they understand clearly what is being communicated, they are much more likely to ask for clarification or repetition than a younger person. Once they do think that they understand the information, they may rephrase it so that the health care professional has the opportunity to correct any misconceptions.

If the older adult is rushed or upset, however, he or she may not ask for reassurance about what has just been communicated, and may leave the situation misunderstanding the information.

The implications that this has for communicating health information to older adults include the following:

- Older adults may require reassurance that the information they have just learned is correct.

- In a rushed or emotionally charged situation, the older adult may not ask for reassurance about new information, and may leave the situation with an incorrect or incomplete understanding.

Section 18
Older Adult Learning Factor: Use of Appropriate Examples in Aiding Learning

Many older adults benefit by hearing examples that illustrate their cases in terms of treatments or lifestyle changes.

Background

Older adults want reassurance that their health condition is not unique. They learn more about their case if it is compared with another person's situation (anonymously, of course) similar in details to theirs. This is why a number of health web sites as well as paper publications designed especially for older adults use personal scenarios to teach about health conditions. The older adult can then find someone "like me" and learn about how that person is managing similar conditions or diseases.

One implication that this has for communicating health information to older adults is the following:

- Older adults want examples of how other older adults deal with certain conditions or diseases. This helps them to learn new information about their own conditions in a personal context, rather than in the abstract.

Section 19
Older Adult Learning Factor: Role of Cause and Effect in Learning

Many older adults benefit by hearing what the causes and effects are of particular lifestyle changes or treatment options.

Background

Many older adults, particularly those of the "baby boom" generation, are much more active in managing their health care than those of their parents' and grandparents' generations. They want to have a role in health care decisions, and are much more likely to want to discuss options rather than accept the ruling of their health care professionals without question. One factor that plays an important role in older adult learning and decision-making is knowledge of the causes and effects of conditions and diseases. This can include discussing how an individual's lifestyle can lead to a particular condition (smoking leading to heart disease, for example; or obesity contributing to Type II diabetes), and how a lifestyle change can help to prevent or, at the very least, mitigate the effects of a disease or condition.

The implications that this has for communicating health information to older adults include the following:

- Older adults, particularly those aged 55 - 65, want to have an active role in managing their health care and in making health-related decisions.

- Older adults benefit from health education by learning the causes and effects of diseases and conditions. This information is useful in helping them to make informed decisions about their health and their lifestyles.

Resources

Section 1:
A Focus on the Issues

1. MEDLINEplus (*medlineplus.gov*) is the premiere consumer web site developed and maintained by the National Library of Medicine at the National Institutes of Health. It has information on medications, health, diseases, clinical trials, medical references and much more. It can be searched in a variety of ways, including key words and alphabetical lists.

2. Food Safety Web Page for Seniors (*http:// vm.cfsan.fda.gov/~dms/seniorsd.html*). This web page is jointly sponsored by the Food and Drug Administration and AARP.

3. Centers for Disease Control and Prevention (*www.cdc.gov*). This web site has health information for seniors, as well as news about immunizations.

4. National Institute on Aging health information (*www.nia.nih.gov/data/pbusearch.asp*). It is possible to access the AgePages from this part of the NIA site. AgePages are written for older adults and caregivers on a variety of pertinent health topics.

5. Publications for Older People from the U.S. Food and Drug Administration (*http://www.fda.gov/oc/*

olderpersons/olderpubs.html#fs). Publications on arthritis, cancer, nutrition, medical treatments, women's health, and osteoporosis.

6. *Exercise: A Guide from the National Institute on Aging* (NIA) from NIH (Publication Number NIH 99-4258). Order from:
   NIAIC
   Department W
   P.O. Box 8057
   Gaithersburg, MD 20898-8057

7. *To Your Health! Food Safety for Seniors.* USDA and FDA. October 2000. Available in PDF format at *http://www.foodsafety.gov/~fsg/sr2.html.*

Section 2:
Self-directed Learning

1. *www.clinicaltrials.gov*: Government web site with a list of current clinical trials.

2. *www.medlineplus.gov*: The government health web site for consumers hosted by the National Library of Medicine at NIH.

3. *www.healthfinder.gov*: The government health web site hosted by the U.S. Department of Health and Human Services.

Section 3:
Social Learning Context

1. *http://www.nhlbi.nih.gov/hbp/index.html.* Guide for lowering high blood pressure from the National Heart, Lung, and Blood Institute.

2. *www.medlineplus.gov.* Consumer health web site from the National Library of Medicine. Information on clinical trials, general health, diseases, and medications.

3. *www.nih.gov.* Main web site for the National Institutes of Health. All the institutes under this umbrella can be accessed from the home page of the NIH site.

4. *www.cdc.gov.* Main web site for the Centers for Disease Control and Prevention. Information on diseases, health, prevention, and immunizations.

Section 4:
Reliance on Third-Party Validation

1. How to Talk to Your Doctor: *www.aarp.org/confacts/health/talkdr.html*

2. *www.nih.gov.* Main web site for the National Institutes of Health. All the institutes under this umbrella can be accessed from the home page of the NIH site.

3. *www.cdc.gov.* Main web site for the Centers for Disease Control and Prevention. Information on diseases, health, prevention, and immunizations.

4. *www.healthfinder.gov.* Main consumer health web site from the U.S. Department of Health and Human Services. Now available in a Spanish version.

Section 5:
Chance to Practice and Review

1. *www.nih.gov/nia.* National Institute on Aging.

2. *http://www.nhlbi.nih.gov/hbp/index.html.* Your Guide to Lowering High Blood Pressure.

3. *Exercise: A Guide from the National Institute on Aging,* Public Information Office, National Institute on Aging, National Institutes of Health, Publication No. NIH 99-4258.

4. *http://www.aoa.gov/elderpage.html#ap.* AgePages from the National Institute on Aging. Long list of topics related to aging matters.

Section 6:
Desire for Hands-On Learning

1. National Council on Patient Information and Education (NCPIE): *www.talkaboutrx.org*.

2. *http://www.umassmed.edu/diabeteshandbook/ chap05.htm#Instructions*. University of Massachusetts Medical School web site with instructions for self-monitoring blood glucose.

Section 7:
Request for Memory Prompts

1. Forgetfulness: It's Not Always What You Think. AgePage from the National Institute on Aging. Available online at *http://www.aoa.dhhs.gov/aoa/PAGES/ AGEPAGES/forget.html*.

Section 8:
Need for Facts to Support Treatments

1. Agency for Health Care Policy and Research, Publications Clearinghouse, P.O. Box 8547, Silver Spring, MD 20907, 800-358-9295, *www.ahcpr.gov/consumer*. Source of the following publications: Prescription Medicines and You, Pain Control After Surgery, Be Informed: Questions to Ask Your Doctor Before You Have Surgery.

2. FDA Guide to Choosing Medical Treatments (Reprint 95-1223). Free guide from the Food and Drug Administration, Office of Consumer Inquiries: HFE-88, 5600 Fishers Lane, Rockville, MD 20857, 301-443-3170, *www.fda.gov*.

3. Evaluating Health Information on the WWW: A Guide for Older Adults and Caregivers. (2001). Available in PDF format online from the SPRY Foundation, 10 G Street, NE, Suite 600, Washington, DC. *www.spry.org*.

Section 9:
Use of Body Language/Facial Expressions in Indicating Understanding

1. Heery, Kathleen (2000, June). Straight talk about the patient interview. *Nursing.*

2. Nichols, Ralph G. (1957). *Are You Listening?* New York: McGraw Hill.

Section 10:
Reluctance to Ask Too Many Questions

1. AARP Webplace. *Caregiving: Communicating with Health Professionals, http://www.aarp.org/confacts/caregive/healthprof.html.*

2. Doctor-Patient Communication Tips, Quackwatch *http://www.quackwatch.com/02ConsumerProtection/commtips.html*

3. MEDLINEplus. The consumer web site from the National Library of Medicine, *www.medlineplus.gov.*

Section 11:
Desire for structured and easily understood protocols for lifestyle changes or treatment

1. *http://www.surgeongeneral.gov/tobacco/5dayplan.htm.* This is an example of a clear, easy-to-follow procedure for getting ready to quit smoking.

2. *http://www.consumer.gov/weightloss/setgoals.htm.* Information on how to lose weight.

3. *http://www.americanheart.org/presenter.jhtml?identifier=1330.* These are dietary guidelines that are very clear and easy to follow from the American Heart Association.

Section 12:
Desire to Understand All Options and Alternatives

1. *www.medicare.gov*: Official web site for Medicare information.

2. *www.aoa.gov*: Official web site of the U. S. Administration on Aging. Contains contact information for the state Area Agencies on Aging, including their web sites.

3. *www.medlineplus.gov*: Consumer web site from the National Library of Medicine. Searchable information on health and medications.

4. *www.clinicaltrials.gov*: Government web site listing clinical trials that are looking for test subjects. Describes who is eligible.

5. Agency for Healthcare Research and Quality (2000, February). Now you have a diagnosis, what's next? Publication No. 00-0004.

Section 13:
Distrust/Dislike of Communications Technologies

1. *www.cyberseniors.org*: This is the web site for the group CyberSeniors.org, originally based in Maine, but now spreading to other parts of the country. CyberSeniors provide computer training classes for older adults.

2. *www.seniornet.org*: SeniorNet is an organization that provides computer training for older adults in communities across the nation.

3. *www.oasisnet.org*: The OASIS Institute, sponsored in part by the May Company, has senior centers in department stores in 25 cities around the U.S. Part of their programming is an intergenerational class in which students teach older adults how to use the computer (Bytes Build Bridges).

Section 14:
Opportunity for Reflection

1. Belzer, Ellen J. (1999, May). Improving patient communication in no time. *Family Practice Management.* Available online at *www.aafp.org/fpm/990500fm/23.html.*

Section 15:
Avoiding Overly Technical Terms

1. *www.medlineplus.gov:* Consumer web site of the National Library of Medicine with information on medications.

2. *www.healthfinder.gov:* Consumer web site of the U.S. Department of Health and Human Services with information on medications.

3. *www.nhlbi.nih.gov:* Web site for National Heart, Lung, and Blood Institute. Web site has a section just for older adults with hypertension with information on medications, causes, effects, and lifestyle advice.

4. Merck Index: Publication from Merck Pharmaceuticals with information on all medications.

5. Tips on Communicating with Your Doctor, Council for Older Adults of Delaware County. Available online at *www.growingolder.com,* under "Council Communicator," July/August 2000.

Section 16:
Secure Learning Environment

1. *Patient Education in Your Practice.* Available from the American Academy of Family Physicians (*www.aafp.org/pehandbook/* .)

Section 17:
Importance of Reinforcement

1. *www.medlineplus.gov:* Consumer health web site from

the National Library of Medicine. Contains basic explanations of how the body works, as well as how medications work in the body.

2. *www.fda.gov*: Official web site of the U.S. Food and Drug Administration. Contains special brochures on Food Safety and Nutrition for older adults.

Section 18:
Use of Appropriate Examples in Aiding Learning

1. *www.Seniors.gov*: Federal government's web site for older adults.

2. *www.nhlbi.nih.gov*: Official web site for the National Heart, Lung, and Blood Institute at NIH.

3. *www.aoa.gov*: Official web site for the U.S. Administration on Aging.

4. *www.nia.nih.gov*: Official web site for the National Institute on Aging at NIH (home of AgePages)

5. Food Safety for Seniors: Publication from the U.S.D.A. and Food and Drug Administration.

Section 19:
Role of Cause and Effect in Learning

1. Kahn, R. and Rowe, J. *Successful Aging* (2000). Book explaining the science behind successful aging. Based upon a study of aging funded by the MacArthur Foundation.

2. *www.medlineplus.gov*: Consumer web site from the National Library of Medicine with explanations of how the body works, how diseases affect the body, and how medications work in the body.

3. *www.healthfinder.gov*: Consumer web site from the U.S. Department of Health and Human Services. Basic health information, plus a version in Spanish.

Communicating With Older Adults

References

Section 1:
A Focus on the Issues

Conaway, F. (1997, July). Primelife top 10 tips for selling to the mature market. *American Salesman*, 42(7), 9-13.

Maehr, M.L. & Braskamp, L.A. (1986). *The motivation factor: A theory of personal investment*. Lexington, MA: Lexington.

Nordstrom, A.D. (1997, September 15). Adult students a valuable market to target. *Marketing News*, 31(19), 20.

Section 2:
Self-directed Learning

Knowles, M. (1973). Toward a model of lifelong education. *The adult learner: A neglected species*, pp. 159-163. Huston, TX: Gulf Publishing Company.

Ingalls, J. (1999, Spring). Andragogy concepts for adult learning. *Readings for Self-Assessment*. Boston, MA: Wheatly Copy Store.

Schulz, R. & Heckhausen, J. (1991, Winter). Adult development, control and adaptive functioning. *Journal of Social Issues*, 41(4), 177-196.

Section 3:
Social Learning Context

Gage, F.H. & Kempermann, G. (1999, May). New nerve cells for the adult brain. *Scientific American*, 280(5), 38-43.

Gamache, S. (1997). Reaching High-Risk Groups. In A. E. Cote (Ed.), *Fire Protection Handbook*, 18th Ed., Quincy, MA: National Fire Protection Association.

Glass, J.C., Jr. (1996). Factors affecting learning in older adults. *Educational Gerontology*, 22(4), 359-372.

Ingalls, J. (1999, Spring). Andragogy Concepts for Adult Learning. *Readings for Self-Assessment*. Boston, MA: Wheatly Copy Store.

Schaie, K.W. (1995, May). Mind exercises to keep you sharp. *New Choices for Retirement Living*, 35(4), 22-24.

Section 4:
Reliance on Third Party Validation

Consumers' Research Magazine. (1997, Jan.). More HMO information needed for seniors. *Consumers' Research Magazine*, 80(1), 28-31.

Gentry, J. W., Kennedy, P. and Macintosh, G. (1995). Marketing implications of the expected role of physicians in family decisions concerning the institutionalization of the elderly. *Psychology and Marketing*, 12, 647-662.

Glass, J.C., Jr. (1996). Factors affecting learning in older adults. *Educational Gerontology*, 22(4), 359-372.

Section 5:
Chance to Practice and Review

Glass, J.C., Jr. (1996). Factors affecting learning in older adults. *Educational Gerontology*, 22(4), 359-372.

Truluck, J.E. & Courtenay, B.C. (1999, April/May). Learning style preferences among older adults. *Educational Gerontology*, 25(3), 221-236.

Section 6:
Desire for Hands-On Learning

Patlack, M. (January/February 1991). Oz fun but home comfier: Older adults examine healthcare options. *FDA Consumer*.

Truluck, J.E. & Courtenay, B.C. (1999, April/May). Learning style preferences among older adults. *Educational Gerontology*, 25(3), 221-236.

Section 7:
Request for Memory Prompts

Craik, F.I.M. & Jennings, J.M. (1992). Human Memory, pp. 51-83. In Craik, F.I.M., and Salthouse, T. (Eds.), *The Handbook of Aging and Cognition*. Hillsdale, NJ: Erlbaum.

Glass, J.C., Jr. (1996). Factors affecting learning in older adults. *Educational Gerontology*, 22(4), 359-372.

TenHouten, W. (1997). Neurosociology. *Journal of Social & Evolutionary Systems*, 20(1), 7–37.

Zarit, S.H. (1982, August). Memory training for severe memory loss: Effects on senile dementia patients and their families. *The Gerontologist*, 22(4), 373-377.

Section 8:
Need for Facts to Support Treatments

Agency for Health Care Policy and Research. (July 1999). *Choosing Treatments*. Retrieved from *www.ahcpr.gov/consumer/qntascii/quttreat.htm*.

Meyer, B.J.F., Russo, C. & Talbot, A. (1995). Discourse comprehension and problem solving: Decisions about the treatment of breast cancer by women across the life span. *Psychology and Aging*, 10(1), 84-103.

Section 9:
Use of Body Language/Facial Expressions in Indicating Understanding

Boyd, S. D. (May, 1998). Listen up! *Nursing*, 28(5),60.

Duffy, F.D. (October 28, 2000). How to counsel patients about exercise: an office-friendly approach. *Physician and Sportsmedicine*, pp. 53-8.

Festa, L. (2000). Maximizing learning outcomes by videotaping nursing students' interaction with a standardized patient. *Journal of Psychosocial Nursing and Mental Health Services.* 38(5), 37.

Findlay, D. (1987). Body Language. *Australian Family Physician*, 16(3), 229-236.

Section 10:
Reluctance to Ask Too Many Questions

Brock, F. (February 4, 2001). *Talking Back is Good Medicine*, New York Times.

Section 11:
Desire for Appropriate and Easily Understood Information on Lifestyle Changes or Treatment

Glass, J.C., Jr. (1996). Factors affecting learning in older adults. *Educational Gerontology*, 22(4), 359-372.

Kolb, D.A. (1984). *Experiential learning: Experience as the source of learning and development.* Englewood Cliffs, NJ: Prentice-Hall.

Meyer, B.J.F., Russo, C. & Talbot, A. (1995). Discourse comprehension and problem solving: Decisions about the treatment of breast cancer by women across the life span. *Psychology and Aging*, 10(1), 84-103.

Truluck, J.E. & Courtenay, B.C. (1999, April/May). Learning style preferences among older adults. *Educational Gerontology*, 25(3), 221-236.

Section 12:
Desire to Understand All the Options and Alternatives

Guy, B.S. & Rittenburg, T.L. (1994, Jan./Feb.). Dimensions and characteristics of time perceptions and perspectives among older consumers. *Psychology & Marketing*, 11(1), 35-56.

Puopolo, A. L. (July 1999). Gaining confidence to talk about end-of-life care. *Nursing*, 29(7), 49-51.

Smyer, M.A. (1993, Winter/Spring). Aging and decision-making capacity. *Generations: The Journal of the Western Gerontological Society*, 17(1).

Section 13:
Dislike/Distrust of Communications Technologies

Auletta, K. & Gilder, G. (1995, Mar./Apr.). Focal point on convergence. *Educom Review*, 30 (2), 20-23.

Czaja, S. J., Guerrier, J.H., Nair, S.N., & Landauer, T.K. (1993). Computer communications as an aid to independence for older adults. *Behavior and Information Technology* 12(4), 197-207.

Diehl, M. (1998, August). Everyday competence in later life: Current status and future directions. *The Gerontologist*, 38(4), 422-433.

Forbes, S. & Hoffart, N. (1998, Nov.). Elders' decision-making regarding the use of long-term care services: A precarious balance. *Qualitative Health Research*, 8(6), 736-750.

Kane, B. & Sands, D.Z. (1998). Guidelines for the clinical use of electronic mail with patients. The AMIA Internet Working Group, Task Force on Guidelines for the Use of Clinic-Patient Electronic Mail. *Journal of the American Medical Information Association*, 5: 104-111.

Mandl, K. D., Kohane, I. S., Brandt, A. M. (1998, Sept. 15). Electronic patient-physician communication: problems and promise. *Annals of Internal Medicine*, 129: 495-500.

Section 14:
Opportunity for Reflection

Fischman, J. (2000, January 31). Get better care by being a little pushy with your doctor. *U. S. News & World Report*.

Strauss, B.S. (1998, April 13). Unconventional wisdom keeps my waiting room full. *Medical Economics.*

Truluck, J.E. & Courtenay, B.C. (1999, April/May). Learning style preferences among older adults. *Educational Gerontology,* 25(3), 221-236.

Section 15:
Avoiding Overly Technical Terms

Schaie, K.W. & Willis, S.L. (1996). Life-span development: Implications for education. *Review of Research in Education,* 6, 120-156.

Author. (2001, Jan.) Low health literacy harms patient health, increases health care costs. *Views Making News,* 2(1), 1, 15.

Section 16:
Secure Learning Environment

Belzer, E. J. (1999, May). Improving patient communication in no time. *Family Practice Management.*

Charnow, J. A. (1998). Study reveals value of small talk with patients. *Medical Tribune*: Internist and Cardiologist Edition, 39(16): 2.

Cotter, K. L. and Hoffman, W. M. (1997, July/August). A sure way to revive the physician-patient relationship. *Family Practice Management.*

Glass, J.C., Jr. (1996). Factors affecting learning in older adults. *Educational Gerontology,* 22(4), 359-372.

Guldan S. and Hui, W. (2000). New directions in communicating better nutrition to older adults. *Journal of Community Nutrition,* 2(1).

Lieberman, J.A. (2000, May/June). Using the BATHE technique with older adult patients. *Geriatric Times,* 1(1).

Mann, Denise. (1998). Doctors, patients need to talk more. *Medical Tribune*: Family Physician Edition, 39(1): Jobson Healthcare Group.

McCulloch, J., Ramesar, S. & Peterson, H. (1998, May). Psychotherapy in primary care: The BATHE technique. *American Family Physician*, retrieved from *www.aafp.org*.

Strauss, B. S. (1998). Unconventional wisdom keeps my waiting room full. *Medical Economics*.

Section 17:
Importance of Reinforcement

Glass, J.C., Jr. (1996). Factors affecting learning in older adults. *Educational Gerontology*, 22(4), 359-372.

Section 18:
Use of Appropriate Examples in Aiding Learning

TenHouten, W. (1997). Neurosociology. *Journal of Social & Evolutionary Systems*, 20(1), 7–37.

Section 19:
Role of Cause and Effect in Learning

Glass, J.C., Jr. (1996). Factors affecting learning in older adults. *Educational Gerontology*, 22(4), 359-372.

Appendix:
Comparison of Strategies Used by Older Learners and Younger Learners

Finding (Older Adults) **Sources**: *Bridging Principles of Older Adult Learning*	Comparison to Children **Sources:** *See Bibliography, starting on page 116*	Implications for Communication and Instruction for Older Adults
There are links between stimulating environments, continued growth of older adult brain cells, and learning and memory.	There are links between stimulating environments and development of learning and memory skills.	Instruction should take place in stimulating environments; e.g. hands-on settings, group learning, high interactivity with the curriculum, many and varied visuals, tailored feedback, intergenerational situations, etc.
Older adults develop compensatory strategies – as some learning functions wear down, others take over.	Children develop compensatory strategies for areas of deficit (illiteracy; innumeracy; vision problems; hearing problems). This ability to compensate can be used to both the individual's advantage and disadvantage as he/she ages.	Instruction needs to be designed for a variety of compensatory methods. For example, if an older adult has memory problems, he/she should be able to access reminders/content as many times as necessary in the course of performing a task or learning a skill. Those who are visual learners, yet have reduced eyesight, should be provided with larger text and images, as well as auditory back-up.

Finding (Older Adults)	Comparison to Children	Implications for... Older Adults
Older adults use their experience, skills, and knowledge in processing new information and making decisions.	Children build their experience, knowledge, and skills through processing new information and making decisions.	Instruction/communication needs to take into account that older adults base their learning and decisions on a lifetime of experience, knowledge, and skills. This may mean that they can enter instruction at a higher level than younger people. It can also mean, if their existing knowledge base in some areas is flawed, they may need to "unlearn" and "relearn" some concepts. Pre-assessments can help to determine an older adult's entry level into instruction.
Strategies for encoding, storage, and retrieval of information can help older adults learn effectively.	Children learn most effectively, and can transfer their learning strategies to new areas, when they are made aware of how they encode, store, and retrieve information (metacognition).	Instruction for older adults should include guidance on how to encode, store, and retrieve new information. This may take the form of using mnemonics or icons to stimulate recall and recognition.

Finding (Older Adults)	Comparison to Children	Implications for... Older Adults
Lifelong learning stimulates the cognitive process in older adults and provides them with a sense of control over their environment.	Children can be taught in a manner that supports the concept of life-long learning as a normal and desirable process. It is important to instill the thought that learning does not end with formal schooling.	Communication/instruction for older adults should be structured to promote curiosity and learning. The communication should not merely "feed" information to the older adult, but stimulate the learning of that and related information. Asking the question, "Want to know more?" as an option on CD-ROMs and web sites is an example of how to extend opportunities for learning.
Research is demonstrating the importance of third-party validation in helping older adults make decisions.	Children begin by using people they perceive as "experts" to validate information. For young children, these experts are parents and teachers. As children mature, they have a tendency to believe what is in the news as factual, or what a "hero" (such as a sports figure or actor) represents as true.	In crafting instruction for older adults, it is important to allow for third-party validation of the information. This could include such activities as group instruction; providing web sites with links to reliable, content-based websites; providing toll-free numbers to call with "experts" on the other end of the line to answer questions; and other methods older adults can use to validate information.

Finding (Older Adults)	Comparison to Children	Implications for... Older Adults
The degree of environmental complexity in older adults' lives has a direct impact on their learning and decision-making.	Children, even the very youngest, react to the stimuli provided by their environments. If the environment is stimulating and exciting, children respond by developing at a normal, or above normal pace. Non-stimulating environments slow down or stunt children's development.	In crafting instruction for older adults, the learning environment must be taken into consideration. The environment should allow for a high degree of interactivity and feedback. This is particularly true in crafting web-based instructional programs, where the older learner might be working on his or her own. The web-based instruction should be as interactive as possible, and allow the older learner to track his or her progress along the way.
Learning requires a good fit between the competencies of the individual and the demands of the environment.	This is essentially the same for children, who can be discouraged when the learning challenge is too great for their abilities, but bored if the learning situation is not challenging at all.	It is important, in instruction and communication, to assess the abilities and competencies of the older adult learner before designing the instruction or communication piece. Adults can be pre-assessed for their knowledge and skills, as well as their preferred styles of learning. Some adults, for example, prefer self-directed, individualized learning; while others learn best in interactive groups or by working peer-to-peer. Since it is often difficult to determine the group members' learning styles when they arrive for a course, it is —>

Finding (Older Adults)	Comparison to Children	Implications for... Older Adults
		important to build alternative instructional delivery methods into a course or educational materials. For example, health information for older adults can be delivered in a workshop setting, through a video, on the Web, or in print. This gives the older learner the opportunity to match his/her learning style and ability level to the best mode of instruction. It is also important to structure educational materials so that the older adult learners can take alternate pathways through the material. Learners knowledgeable in a particular subject, for example, may choose to skip the basics and take a more accelerated route. Beginning learners in a subject may need to repeat sections, or to practice a skill before moving on.

Finding (Older Adults)	Comparison to Children	Implications for... Older Adults
Older adults have five areas of need for learning: 1. Coping needs (skills to meet daily demands) 2. Expressive needs (means for creative expression) 3. Contributive needs (giving back to the community) 4. Influence needs (exercising control over the environment) 5. Need for transcendence (rising above the mundane requirements of day-to-day activity through spirituality)	Children typically concentrate their learning needs in coping (learning the basic skills to survive in an adult world) and expressing themselves. As they get older, they perceive the value of giving to their communities, controlling their environment, and becoming involved in spiritual activities. This movement fits with Piaget's work in that young children move from a "me-focused" life (pre-operational through concrete operational stages) to the formal operational stage. In this last stage (from approximately 14 years and older), children are able to think in the abstract, and see their existence as part of the greater whole.	It is important when designing instruction for older adults to consider the needs of the adults receiving the instruction. If the instruction is to meet a coping need, it should be highly focused and to the point. Other needs, however, such as expressive and contributive, require a more open-ended approach to learning. They may also require a greater level of interactivity and reflection. This may mean that instruction designed to meet these latter needs requires more time than instruction for coping needs.

Finding (Older Adults)	Comparison to Children	Implications for... Older Adults
Culture and gender play a role in the cognitive processes of older adults.	This is the same with children. It has been well documented that girls learn many types of skills and knowledge more quickly than boys at an early age, but boys do catch up as they mature. In addition, children's cultures that value education highly provide more support for learning than cultures that do not value education as highly.	In designing effective instruction or communication pieces for older adults, it is important to: • Take language differences into account (e.g., Spanish or Chinese versions in areas of high Hispanic and/or Chinese populations). • Take cultural differences in learning styles into account (e.g., Japanese schooling, with a strong emphasis on studying for long hours in classrooms of as many as 50 students, is very different from the U.S. or U.K. system). • Take gender differences into consideration (e.g., men typically prefer learning alone with lectures, audiotapes or reading, while women typically prefer learning through group discussions and a generally more interactive environment).

Finding (Older Adults)	Comparison to Children	Implications for... Older Adults
Beliefs and attitudes about memory (metamemory) have a significant impact on cognitive functioning.	Younger people are typically trained in memory tasks and in the use of mnemonics in such formal courses as mathematics (times tables, geometric postulates); English (rules of grammar); geography (names of places); history (facts and dates); science (names of body parts, laws of physics); music (types of notes). While these tasks are classic memory-builders with young people, the memory skills developed in the learning process have a tendency to get discarded with age.	In designing instruction, it is important to instill in older adults the feeling that they *can* remember such things as the steps of tasks they are learning to perform (self-efficacy). This feeling can be developed and reinforced by the opportunity to practice the task as many times as necessary, and to apply the skills learned from the task to a new situation as soon as possible. The feeling can also be strengthened by the use of memory monitoring tactics, memory clues, or refresher options. For example, an online curriculum to teach an older adult how to search a particular web site can have an option for a review built in each time the older adult accesses the curriculum.

Finding (Older Adults)	Comparison to Children	Implications for... Older Adults
Learning styles and literacy levels are important features of the successful acquisition of knowledge.	Children's learning styles continue to jell throughout the formal educational process. It is important, in working with children, to give them opportunities to learn in a variety of ways so that they recognize how they learn the best. Literacy levels are dependent upon the child's intelligence, the type of reading instruction provided, the child's developmental readiness for the reading instruction, practice, and follow-up at home. Other factors in literacy levels include the presence or absence of learning disabilities. If the factors that hinder literacy are not addressed in childhood, the illiteracy will continue to be a factor in adulthood and older adulthood.	In preparing instruction and/or communication pieces for older adults, both learning styles and literacy levels need to be taken into consideration. In developing a print piece for the older adults in the general population, it is vital to pilot test the reading level of the piece with a large sample of the target audience. It may also be necessary to use many graphics to assist those who have a low literacy level.

To address different learning styles, instruction and/or communication pieces can be offered in a variety of formats: online, video, audio, demonstration, classes, print, etc. The more widely used the communications piece is expected to be, the more format options should be available. |

Finding (Older Adults)	Comparison to Children	Implications for... Older Adults
The convergence of television, computers and technologically mediated learning will aid in the education of older adults.	This finding is true for children as well, but there is concern in the educational field that children may not be getting enough hands-on experience to build concepts – virtual experience is not enough. But there are also positive aspects of learning technology: • Providing experiences that are too expensive, dangerous, or impossible to provide "live". • Allowing children to self-pace their learning. • Providing children with instant feedback on a task.	Educational technology provides a new frontier for older adult learning in that the availability of the delivery platforms (televisions, VCRs, computers, etc.) is much more widespread in homes than it has been in the past. In addition, the existence of the World Wide Web provides content for older adults that they may not have been able to afford or access in the past. Educational technology also allows an older adult to work at his or her own pace, to work during "off hours," to assess his or her own progress, and to choose the content that is most interesting and desirable. Instruction/communication pieces that depend upon educational technology, however, must take the following into consideration: • Availability of the technology to the target audience • Cost of the technology • Interactivity of the technology • Human factors aspects (how people are able to access and use the technology, for example)

Finding (Older Adults)	Comparison to Children	Implications for... Older Adults
There are seven areas that must be addressed when looking at factors that affect older adult learning: 1. changes in physical capacities 2. changes in sensory capacities 3. changes related to speed and timing 4. attitudinal changes 5. learning capacity and performance 6. changes in memory 7. changes in adjustment abilities and morale	The seven areas outlined for older adults have parallels in how children learn: 1. stage of physical capacity (developmental readiness) 2. deficiencies in sensory capacities for which children must compensate 3. capacity to pace work 4. developing attitudes 5. ability to learn in the first place (mental capacity) 6. ability to build memory skills 7. ability to adjust to the control of the adult world	Implications for instruction include: • avoidance of long learning sessions • capacity for self-paced instruction • stress-free learning situations • minimized demands for speed • more structured activity • comfortable, non-threatening environment • presence of friends or family members in learning environment • early success in the instruction • building on older adults' skills and abilities • meaningful and relevant tasks • reassurance of their abilities • peer teaching • memory cues • time for practice and rehearsal • links to relevant experiences • organizing strategies and frequent summations • many opportunities to develop abilities • reinforcement of competencies • assistance in coping with changes

Finding (Older Adults)	Comparison to Children	Implications for... Older Adults
Many older adults are "centered" with an outwardly directed, altruistic orientation.	Children are "centered" toward themselves, at least until they reach the stage of later concrete and early formal operations.	Instruction for older adults should be designed to show clear connections between what they are learning and its impact on the outside world (lives of others). An example of how to do this could be the inclusion of flow charts in curricula, showing how others use similar skills and information in their lives. In dealing with instruction on smoking cessation, for example, a flow chart could show the effects that continued smoking has on others, as well as the effects that ceasing smoking has on others.
Older adults have strong emotional bonds toward other people, objects, and beliefs.	In early life, children begin to develop bonds to other people, objects, and beliefs, and they learn what happens, emotionally, when those bonds are broken.	One way to build upon older adults' strong emotional bonds to others is to use case studies of "real people" to illustrate concepts and to develop skills. The National Heart, Lung, and Blood Institute used this approach with their high blood pressure website, relating the stories of five people to show how to identify, deal with, and prevent high blood pressure.

Finding (Older Adults)	Comparison to Children	Implications for... Older Adults
Older adults are motivated to learn so they can better adapt to their environment (fulfill their recognized needs and cope with life's challenges).	Children are often motivated to learn to satisfy their curiosity and to fulfill the requirements of those in authority (parents, guardians, and teachers).	In designing instruction for older adults, it is important to ensure that they see a clear connection between the concepts and/or skills being taught and their needs and challenges. For example, in teaching an older adult how to navigate a website, it is crucial to demonstrate how this skill will help him or her to find information on any website that can solve health (or other) problems, or just to keep the adult up-to-date with the world.

Bibliography for Children's Learning Styles

Andersson, B. (1990). Pupils' conceptions of matter and its transformations (age 12-16). In P. Lijnse, P. Licht, W. de Vos, & A.J. Waarlo (Eds.), *Relating macroscopic phenomena to microscopic particles* (pp. 12-35). Utrecht: CD-þ Press.

Bar, V. (1989). Children's views about the water cycle. *Science Education,* 73, 481-500.

Bar, V. (1986). *The development of the conception of evaporation.* The Amos de-Shalit Science Teaching Centre in Israel, The Hebrew University of Jerusalem, Israel.

Barker, M. (1985). Teaching and Learning About Photosynthesis, Science Education Research Unit, Working Papers 220-229, University of Waikato, Hamilton, New Zealand.

Bell, B., & Brook, A. (1984). *Aspects of secondary students' understanding of plant nutrition.* Leeds, UK: University of Leeds, Centre for Studies in Science and Mathematics Education.

Bernstein, A.C., & Cowan, P.A. (1975). Children's concepts of how people get babies. *Child Development, 46,* 77-91.

Black, Paul., & Solomon, J. (1983). Life world and science world: Pupils' ideas about energy. In G. Marx (Ed.), *Entropy in the school: Proceedings of the 6th Danube seminar on physics education* (pp. 43-55). Budapest: Roland Eotvos Physical Society.

Blum, L.H. (1977). Health information via mass media: Study of the individual's concepts of the body and its parts. *Psychological Reports, 40,* 991-999.

Bransford, J. D., Brown, A. L., & Cocking, R. R. (Eds.) (1999). *How People Learn.* Washington, DC: National Academy Press.

Brumby, M. (1982). Students' perceptions of the concept of life. *Science Education, 66,* 613-622.

Clough, E.E., & Wood-Robinson, C. (1985b). Children's understanding of inheritance. *Journal of Biological Education, 19,* 304-310.

Driver, R. (1989). *Students' conceptions and the learning of science: Introduction.* International Journal of Science Education, 11(5): 481-490.

Driver, R., Squires, A., Rushworth, P., & Wood-Robinson, V. (1994). *Making Sense of Secondary Science: Research into Children's Ideas.* London: Routledge.

Gellert, E. (1962). Children's conceptions of the content and functions of the human body. *Genetic Psychology Monographs, 65,* 293-305.

Harlen, W. (1988). *The Teaching of Science.* London: Fulton.

Hewson, P.W., & Thorley, N. R. (1989). The conditions of conceptual change in the classroom. *International Journal of Science Education*, 11(5): 541-553.

Lederman, Norman. (1992). Students' and teachers' conceptions of the nature of science: A review of the research. *Journal of Research in Science Teaching*, 29, 331-359.

Minstrell, J. (1989). Teaching science for understanding. In L. Resnick & L. Klopfer (Eds.), *Toward the thinking curriculum: Current cognitive research* (pp. 129-149). Alexandria, VA: Association for Supervision and Curriculum Development.

National Research Council (1996). *National Science Education Standards.* Washington, DC: National Academy Press.

Novak, J. D. & Gowin, D. B. (1984). *Learning How to Learn.* Cambridge: Cambridge University Press.

Osborne, R.J., & Freyberg, P. (1985). *Learning in Science: The Implications of 'Children's Science'.* New Zealand: Heinemann.

Pfundt, H. (1981). *Pre-instructional conceptions about substances and transformations of substances*, in Jung, W., Pfundt, H., & von Rhoneck, C. (Eds.), Proceedings of the International Workshop on Problems Concerning Students' Representation of Physics and Chemistry Knowledge, 14–16 September, Pedagogische Hochschule, Ludwigsburg, 320–341.

Piaget, J. (1952). *The Origins of Intelligence in Children.* New York: International Universities Press.

Project 2061, American Association for the Advancement of Science. (1993). *Benchmarks for Science Literacy.* New York: Oxford University Press.

Sere, M. (1982). A study of some frameworks of the field of mechanics used by children (aged 11-13) when they interpret experiments about air pressure. *European Journal of Science Education*, 7(1), 83-93.

Solomon, J. (1983). Learning about energy: How pupils think in two domains. *European Journal of Science Education*, 5, 49-59.

Solomon, J. (1983). Messy, contradictory and obstinately persistent: a study of children's out of school ideas about energy. *School Science Review*, 65 (231): 225 – 33.

Trowbridge, J., & Mintzes, J. (1985). Students' alternative conceptions of animals and animal classification. *School Science and Mathematics*, 85, 304-316.

Watts, M. (1983b). A study of school children's alternative frameworks of the concept of force. *European Journal of Science Education*, 5, 217-230.

ABOUT THE AUTHOR

Ann E. Benbow, Ph.D.

Ann Benbow, Director of Adult Learning and Technology for the SPRY Foundation, is an experienced researcher, curriculum developer, teacher, and trainer. After teaching in high school, elementary school, two-year college, and university, she worked in research and development for the Education Division of the American Chemical Society for 12.5 years. During that time, she was the editor of *WonderScience* magazine, Principal Investigator on NSF projects FACETS, Operation Chemistry Phases I and II, SciTeKS phases I and II, and ScienceGate III and IV. She has also recently co-authored a book on elementary science methods for Wadsworth Publishing (*Elementary Science Education: An Investigation-Based Approach*). In her current position as Director of Adult Learning and Technology at the SPRY Foundation, Dr. Benbow is directing research, curriculum development and training projects related to Successful Aging. One of her roles is Principal Investigator of a new NSF-funded project with the OASIS Institute: *Science Across the Generations*. Her work for many years has involved crafting learning experiences for children and adults that take into account their various learning and communication styles.

Dr. Benbow has a B.S. in Biology from St. Mary's College of Maryland, and a M.Ed. in Science Education and a Ph.D. in Curriculum and Instruction from the University of Maryland College Park.

ABOUT THE SPRY FOUNDATION AND NCPSSM

SPRY Foundation

The **SPRY** (Setting Priorities for Retirement Years) **Foundation** is a 501(c)(3) non-profit research foundation with a mission to promote Successful Aging in the domains of financial security, physical health and wellness, mental health and social environment, and intellectual pursuits. SPRY is the research and education arm of the National Committee to Preserve Social Security and Medicare, and works independently by partnering with organizations to develop and test modules, curricula, training programs, and guides that empower older adults in the four domains. For more information on SPRY's current projects and publications, call (202) 216-0401 or visit *www.spry.org*.

National Committee to Preserve Social Security and Medicare

The National Committee to Preserve Social Security and Medicare is a grassroots advocacy and education association, with millions of members and supporters, dedicated to protecting these entitlements earned by all Americans. The National Committee is a nonprofit, nonpartisan, tax-exempt organization independent of Congress or any government agency. For more information on the National Committee, call (202) 216-0420 or (800) 966-1935, or visit *www.ncpssm.org*.

ABOUT CARESOURCE AND SENIORCLIX

Caresource Healthcare Communications

Caresource is a Seattle-based publisher specializing in healthcare and senior care education and publications. Founded in 1989, the company serves health care providers, managed care plans, trade and professional associations, and consumers.

Caresource's areas of expertise include: patient, staff, and consumer videos; booklets and brochures; books and manuals published to print, CD-ROM, and the Internet; web site design, hosting, and upkeep; and healthcare newsletters and eMagazines.

SeniorClix

SeniorClix is Caresource's consumer-oriented web site. This site is an information and resource pool for older adults, their families, and the senior services health care network. Among the many features are: free forms for health care planning; a collection of national, state and local directories; and a wide range of articles of interest to seniors and those who help care for them.

More information is available at *www.caresource.com* and *www.SeniorClix.com*.

	DATE DUE		